The Enneagram World of the Child

You make me want to be a better man.

Melvin (Jack Nicholson) to Carol (Helen Hunt)
As Good as It Gets

Love inspires us toward authenticity and unity.

John Harper

When you're a parent, everything's on you.

Gary (Vee) Vaynerchuk

The Enneagram World of the Child

Nurturing Resilience and Self-compassion in Early Life

These two qualities—resilience and self-compassion—form the bedrock of healthy psychological development. Everything that follows in this book serves this single purpose: helping our children develop the capacity to bounce back from life's challenges while maintaining a kind and loving relationship with themselves.

John Harper

First Edition: April 2025

ISBN: 979-8-9924438-0-6 (Paperback)

HarpGnosis Books

This book is dedicated to supporting parents and children in their sacred journey of growth and discovery. While the author and publisher have made every effort to ensure the accuracy and completeness of the information in this book, we assume no responsibility for errors, inaccuracies, omissions, or inconsistencies herein.

The Enneagram content in this book draws from the oral tradition and written works of multiple teachers and schools. The author acknowledges this lineage while offering his unique perspective on applying these insights to parenting and child development.

To my children Julia and Devon.
If I had known then what I do now…
But I was not ready for the work or tears.

Love & Remorse

Acknowledgments

A heartfelt thank you to my sister, Catherine Harper, whose keen editorial eye and deep understanding of language and grammar helped shape this book in ways I could not have done alone. Her expertise, generosity, and unwavering support were invaluable throughout this process, offering insightful critiques and thoughtful encouragement at every stage. Beyond technical editing, Catherine brought a rare ability to refine ideas while preserving their essence, ensuring this book remained clear and true to its intent. I am deeply grateful for her time, talent, and dedication—this work is better because of her.

I thank Terrell and Renie for introducing me to the Enneagram and Helen Palmer for her training.

To my many guides and teachers: Michael T., Carole M., Jessica B., David S., Deanne S., Linda K., Patty R., John D., Morton L., and Byron B.

To my friends Holly & Greg B., Anne L., Duncan S., Rennie M., Prakash M., Russ H. Katie V-M., David M., and Rick O., each of you who sat with me in a dyad, triad, and cyclonic that got me this far—your work is not yet done!

But mainly to True Nature, which led me to Together Books in Denver to find **Diamond Heart Book I: Elements of the Real in Man.** And, of course, TN's sidekicks A. H. Almaas (Hameed Ali) and Karen Johnson for pointing the way.

All played a part in helping me to realize:

I can't change, but I can be changed.

Wishing you all bright delight!

Table of Contents

Preface

Most parents have profound hopes and dreams for their children. These aspirations—spoken or unspoken, conscious or unconscious—become one of the most potent forces shaping a child's emerging sense of self and worldview. Your expectations, fears, and need-to-know as a parent silently mold the foundation of your child's experience of who they are and how they relate to life.

At birth, each child presents us with a profound paradox. Though legally a person, they arrive as both a blank canvas awaiting life's impressions and a rich wellspring of untapped potential. These first years of life unfold as a cellular riot of development, a tsunami of sensory stimuli, and the gradual sunrise of a self emerging into the world. While the body arrives fully formed in its basic structure, the self develops gradually through the complex alchemy of biology and environment—and you, the parent, are the primary architect of that environment.

Your Enneagram Type fundamentally shapes how you create your child's Enneagram world of influence. Your particular focus of attention, your characteristic fears and desires, your habitual ways of managing emotions and connection—all these aspects of your Type create the ecosystem in which your child's personality forms. Their emerging patterns are not random developments but intelligent adaptations to your way of being in the world.

Every sight, sound, and touch you provide becomes a brushstroke, painting the foundation of your child's perception. The self emerges slowly, shy at first, as the infant begins to piece together a coherent "I" from scattered fragments of experience. The body serves as a vehicle while the self—soft and malleable—grows within it, shaped by connection, care, and curiosity. A person arises from this intricate dance between nature and nurture—a unique constellation of traits, preferences, and reflections. Yet beneath these layers of personality and self-reflection runs a thread that remains untouched, a quiet essence that was always there before and beyond the story.

The word *person* carries a fascinating lineage that speaks to this interplay between essence and personality. Derived from the Latin *persona*—originally referring to the masks worn by actors in classical theater—it reminds us that the self we present to the world is often a kind of mask shaped by culture, roles, and expectations. Personality becomes our way of navigating life's stage, developing through the imprint of our environment, the stories we internalize, and the conditioning we receive.

Yet personality is not the whole of who we are. Beneath it lies something more fundamental—consciousness, essence, or being—that remains untouched by the shifting roles and facades we adopt. To mistake the face for the mask is to lose sight of the deeper truth of who we and our children are.

The Enneagram offers us a profound map for understanding this territory. More than just a system of nine personality types, it illuminates the patterning of motivations, fears, and desires that drive human behavior while always pointing toward the essence beneath these patterns. Its geometric wisdom reveals how personality patterns are not fixed boxes but dynamic territories that evolve in response to life's challenges and opportunities.

This book explores how your personality patterns create the environment where your child's patterns emerge and develop. It invites you to examine your Type-specific patterns and prejudices, understand how your hopes and fears shape your child's emerging sense of self, and discover ways of parenting that honor the necessity of healthy personality development while maintaining connection to the precious gift of your child's unique essence.

Our journey together will explore practical insights from the Enneagram's wisdom while remaining grounded in the day-to-day reality of raising children. By understanding how your patterns influence your child's development and how you can maintain flexibility rather than rigidity in these patterns, you can help your child develop the resilience and self-compassion they need while maintaining a connection to their authentic nature.

This is not a book about typing children or filtering their unique expression through categorical lenses. Instead, it offers a way of seeing and supporting the delicate process of personality formation while creating space for the mystery of each child's essential being to unfold. I hope these insights will help you navigate the sacred territory of early childhood development with greater awareness, compassion, and wisdom.

Today
the world is birthing you
Yesterday
was the womb of today
As today
is the womb of tomorrow

Today
is the moment to birth
All that yesterday's womb
nurtured in you

Be that majestic generosity
spreading its wings for all.

JH

How to Read This Book

"A journey of a thousand miles begins with a single step."
Lao Tzu

Imagine setting out on a journey across vast waters. Your vessel is well-built, but the key to safe passage lies in the rudder—that seemingly small yet crucial element that determines your course through calm seas and stormy weather. As you begin exploring *The Enneagram World of the Child*, consider this book your rudder, helping you navigate the deep waters of personality development, parental patterns, and the sacred dance of growth between parent and child.

This book is an extended inquiry into the primal forces shaping personality. Like the ocean, these forces are profound, sometimes turbulent, and worthy of careful navigation. Our journey will explore the currents of acceptance, the winds of attachment, the waves of primary emotions, and the deep undertows of the superego—all forces that shape our children's development and our ongoing growth as parents.

Engaging Your Heart and Imagination

In these pages, you're invited into your child's emotional world—where feelings flow like rivers, energy moves like wind, and connection happens through presence rather than words. To enter this world, you'll need to shift from thinking to feeling, from analyzing to experiencing, observing to participating.

The 80/20 Rule of Engagement

To truly benefit from this work, aim to:

- Engage 80% through emotional awareness and bodily sensing
- Use 20% for mental understanding and cognitive reflection

Your child lives in a world of pure emotion and energy. To understand them, you must first reconnect with this way of being.

Throughout these pages, you'll encounter many situations that ask you to imagine yourself in the dynamic dance between parent and child. While the examples feature specific Enneagram Types, the invitation is to place yourself into these scenarios with your unique Type pattern.

- How would your pattern respond?
- What emotions arise?
- What impulses surface?
- What memories stir?

This is not a book to be read but rather a journey to be experienced. Each example, each scenario, each interaction is an invitation to:

- Feel into your immediate emotional response
- Notice sensations in your body
- Connect with your childhood memories
- Sense the energy patterns at play
- Imagine different possibilities

Through this imaginative engagement, you'll begin to loosen rigid patterns and create more space for discovering who your child really is. This isn't about gathering information—it's about developing the emotional flexibility and resilience needed to support your child's authentic development.

Remember: Your child doesn't need you to understand everything intellectually. Your child needs you to be present emotionally, to sense their world from the inside, and to create space for their unique way of being to unfold.

A Note about Typing Children

This book explores how parents' Enneagram patterns influence their children's development. The examples of Emma with Sarah (1), Lucas with Rachel (3), Maya with Priya (5), and others demonstrate how children naturally absorb and respond to their parents' personality patterns. However, it's crucial to understand that this doesn't mean children will develop the identical Enneagram Type as their parents, nor should we attempt to type children.

While children often mirror their parents' beliefs, behaviors, and traits—especially in early development—this mirroring is just one of many complex factors shaping personality formation. A Type Three parent won't necessarily raise a Type Three child, nor will a Type One parent automatically foster Type One patterns in their offspring. The relationship between parent and child patterns is far more nuanced and complex.

The examples in this book illustrate parents' significant role in early development—an aspect of growth where conscious awareness can create meaningful change. By understanding how our patterns influence our children's experiences, we can:

- Work more consciously with our Type's tendencies
- Create space for our children's authentic nature to emerge
- Support healthy development without unconsciously transmitting rigid patterns
- Maintain flexibility in our responses and their growing personalities

The goal isn't to predict or shape our children's eventual Type but to understand how our patterns influence their early development. This understanding allows us to work more consciously with these influences, supporting our children's natural unfolding while maintaining awareness of our own Type's impact.

The examples in this book are meant to illuminate parental influence, not to suggest direct Type transmission from parent to child. By focusing on what we can consciously work with—our patterns and presence—we support our children's authentic development, whatever form that ultimately takes.

The Enneagram World of the Child

The child is born into the physical, emotional, and psychic space created by the parents. In this environment, the child adapts, mirrors, and orients—either aligning with or resisting a parent's influence. In most families, parents have different personality types, so the child has a choice: adopt one, reject one, find a compromise, or live in ambivalence.

But the field is not static. A parent's Enneagram point of fixation (e.g., Type 8) may shift under stress (to Type 5), introducing a new environmental force. Imagine the flux of new parents, their shifting energies shaping the space the child must navigate. This is the dance of adaptation—the unfolding of the child's unique personality.

This book focuses on parents loosening their patterns, not typing their children. Typing a child fixes them in place, reinforcing a specific sense of self rather than presence. The Enneagram is not a tool for control. It is a key to more space, flexibility, and resilience—not rigidity, strategy, and manipulation.

The Structure of Our Journey

We follow five families to illustrate key patterns and developmental dynamics. While the Enneagram system has 36 possible parent combinations, we focus on the Connor, Patel, Chen, Rodriguez, and Smith families. Each represents a different combination of Types and parenting patterns.

See the Appendix for the characteristics of each Enneagram Personality Type and the growth areas for parenting.

Connor Family			
	Sarah (1)	Michael (6)	Emma
Patel Family			
	Priya (5)	Raj (7)	Maya
Chen Family			
	Lisa (8)	David (9)	Marcus
Rodriguez Family			
	Ana (2)	Carlos (4)	Sofia
Smith Family			
	Rachel (3)	James (1)	Lucas

(Enneagram Personality Type in parentheses)

Each chapter unfolds through several essential elements.

Real-Life Observations

As you read on, you're asked to visualize how different families navigate everyday situations and watch their children grow and develop their distinctive personalities:

- Emma working with perfectionist tendencies
- Marcus exploring boundary formation
- Maya developing observation patterns
- Sofia discovering emotional expression
- Lucas learning achievement patterns

You'll recognize deeper currents beneath surface behaviors and understand how:

- Basic patterns emerge
- Development unfolds
- Types form
- Growth occurs

Practical insights will help translate understanding into conscious presence through explorations of how different patterns:

- Express in daily life
- Influence development
- Shape interactions
- Guide growth

Contemplative Elements

Throughout the book, bullet-pointed sections offer "tastes" of different situations and experiences. These aren't lists to quickly scan or mentally check off. They're invitations to pause and feel each moment, to let each point resonate in your body and heart.

Think of each bullet point as a small doorway into the experience. When you encounter them, slow down, take a breath, and let yourself imagine and feel the situation being described. Make it real and personal.

These contemplative moments serve as natural resting places in your journey—safe harbors where you can drop anchor and explore the emotional landscape being revealed. They offer opportunities to:

- Sense your patterns in action
- Feel your child's natural way of being
- Experience your interactions freshly
- Bring your full presence to daily moments

Working with Bullet Points

When you encounter bullet points:

- Pause after each one
- Let the words settle in your body
- Notice what emotions arise
- Allow memories to surface
- Feel how the situation might play out with your child

Remember: Each bullet point is not just information; it's an invitation to experience. Take your time. Let each point speak to you. Real understanding comes not from reading quickly through the list but from letting each element touch you emotionally and energetically.

Navigating This Book

This isn't a book to be rushed through in search of quick answers. Like any meaningful journey across deep waters, it requires patience, attention, and respect for the process. Consider the following guidelines for your exploration.

First Reading

- Take at least a day or two for each chapter
- Read with an open, curious mind
- Notice what resonates and what challenges you
- Begin practicing simple observations
- Keep notes on your discoveries

Second Reading

- Extend over several months as embodied contemplation
- Focus on specific sections that call to you
- Engage in daily contemplation and dialogue
- Practice with greater awareness
- Share discoveries with other parents

As an ongoing exploration, return to relevant sections whenever needed, allowing experience to deepen your understanding as your child progresses through different developmental stages. Engage in continuing dialogue with other parents, sharing insights and perspectives as awareness evolves. Maintain curiosity about recurring patterns and how they manifest at different ages, recognizing that what resonates now may shift as your child grows. Stay open to new possibilities, understanding that development is an ever-unfolding process, and each stage offers fresh opportunities for insight and connection.

The book serves best when insights are shared and discussed. Consider:

- Finding a reading partner
- Joining a parent group
- Sharing observations with your co-parent
- Discussing insights with trusted friends

Through dialogue, we deepen our understanding, share meaningful discoveries, support each other's growth, and maintain momentum in this challenging work. Remember, this journey isn't about reaching a destination but developing awareness and skills for ongoing exploration. Engaging with these concepts allows for deeper integration of insights, the natural development of understanding, genuine pattern recognition, and authentic personal growth alongside your child's development.

A Note on Pattern Recognition

As you read about different personality patterns, you may feel tempted to quickly "type" yourself or your child. Resist this urge. Instead:

- Observe with curiosity
- Notice without judgment
- Stay open to discovery
- Maintain flexible attention

Use the book as a diagnostic tool that serves as a guide for exploration, a map of development, support for growth, and an invitation to presence in your parenting journey. Like any journey across vast waters, this one requires:

- Patience with the process
- Trust in the unfolding
- Respect for the depths
- Commitment to presence

Your willingness to engage deeply with this material and use it as a true rudder for navigation will determine its ability to support your conscious parenting journey.

Introduction

Children are not a distraction from more important work.
They are the most important work.
C.S. Lewis

> Although the heart of this book is the child, it equally speaks about you, the parent. You will have the most influence and impact on your child's development, sense of self, and personality development. The more you explore and work with your understanding of the Enneagram, the more potential and possibilities for resiliency and flexibility in your child's developing personality during this time of maximum plasticity in your child's developing brain and nervous system.

Many, if not most, new parents enter their parenting journey with little understanding of how their patterns shape childhood development. Parenting often begins as an improvisation, guided by instinct and trial and error, rather than an awareness of how your unconscious Type patterns create the environment in which your child's internal world takes shape. Yet, understanding this transmission process is critical to supporting your child's growth in a way that nurtures their individuality while maintaining flexibility in their developing patterns.

Children are not "miniature adults." Their internal world operates on unique rules and rhythms, far removed from the structured logic of adulthood. When you think, "My child is feeling ___," you may be projecting your adult faculties—and your Type's particular focus—into your child's experience. However, depending on their age and developmental stage, they may not yet have fully differentiated their emotions from their sensations and thoughts from their environment. Your Type's approach to emotions, boundaries, and connections creates the landscape in which your child's understanding of themselves unfolds.

It is tempting to assume that because we were all children once, we inherently understand what a child is going through. But having gone through childhood ourselves does not equip us to comprehend it from the perspective of a developing mind, especially since your childhood was shaped by your parents' Type patterns, just as yours are shaping your children. The experiences of a child and those of an adult are not even comparable—more like apples to galaxies than apples to oranges. The sensitivity and impressionability of a child's early life are so profound that they cannot be easily grasped by a mind already shaped by the defenses and conditioning of adulthood.

This profound difference between the world of the child and the world of the adult should be viewed as an invitation, not a barrier, to understanding. It invites you to step outside your Type's habitual frameworks and observe, question, and learn anew. Parenting well is not simply about guiding a child through development but also about allowing the experience of parenting to catalyze your growth and pattern recognition. In their impressionability and openness, children offer a chance to witness life's raw unfolding and rediscover your essential nature beyond your Type's particular focus.

This book is not about "typing" your child or filtering your relationship through the lens of personality categories. It invites understanding of how your patterns influence your child's development, creating the conditions that shape their emerging self. If we type our children, we relate to them as an idea rather than an emerging mystery of being. This becomes another demand and pressure from the family ecosystem to accommodate and conform rather than allowing their authentic nature to unfold. Your role is to witness and support their development with spacious presence, free from the constraints of predetermined categories.

If we type our children, we relate to them as an idea rather than an emerging mystery of being. This becomes another demand and pressure from the family ecosystem to accommodate and conform rather than allowing their authentic nature to unfold. Our role is to witness and support their development with spacious presence, free from the constraints of predetermined categories.

As you read on, you'll "watch" parent-child interactions and see how different Enneagram Types create distinct developmental environments:

> Watch five-year-old Emma at her art table, wholly absorbed in her painting. Her mother Sarah (1) stands in the doorway, feeling the familiar tension between honoring her daughter's creative flow and maintaining the schedule. In this moment, you witness how a Type One parent's patterns around correctness, improvement, and order influence how a child relates to creativity and self-expression.

> Observe four-year-old Maya studying a caterpillar in the garden while her mother Priya (5) manages her own need for space and energy conservation.

This interaction reveals how a Type Five parent's knowledge, withdrawal, and observation patterns shape a child's exploration and connection approach.

Each Type creates a unique developmental landscape:

- Type One parents establish environments of order and improvement
- Type Two parents create atmospheres of emotional attunement and helping
- Type Three parents build worlds of achievement and performance
- Type Four parents foster spaces of emotional depth and authenticity
- Type Five parents develop environments of observation and knowledge
- Type Six parents establish atmospheres of security and preparation
- Type Seven parents create landscapes of possibility and reframing
- Type Eight parents build worlds of protection and strength
- Type Nine parents foster environments of harmony and peace

Your child's emerging patterns aren't random personality traits but sophisticated adaptations to your Type's particular focus, fears, and needs. When Emma carefully erases her drawing, she's not just developing perfectionism—she's adapting to an environment where correctness matters. When Maya observes intensely before engaging, she's not just being cautious—she's mirroring an approach to the world that values understanding before action.

Throughout the following chapters, we'll explore how your Type influences every domain of development—acceptance, attachment, emotions, and other foundational aspects—creating the conditions in which your child's personality forms. Each chapter examines how your pattern shapes a specific aspect of your child's experience and how conscious work with your Type can support healthy development while maintaining flexibility in emerging patterns.

Understanding your Type patterns and how they influence your child's development gives you unprecedented opportunities to support healthy growth while maintaining flexibility in emerging patterns. This book invites you to explore not just your child's development but your patterns as the primary architect of your child's environment.

The Sacred Territory of Early Development

In the beginning, at birth, the child's world is merged with the mother's experience. Her Type pattern fundamentally shapes this early fusion. Watch six-month-old Maya reach her tiny hand toward her mother Priya's (5) face, her wide eyes sparkling with curiosity as Priya instinctively leans in to meet her gaze. Maya giggles, and Priya responds with a gentle smile, their connection flowing in an unbroken dance of need and response. This beautiful fusion of attunement exemplifies how the early world of the child is an inseparable dance from the mother's Type-specific way of engaging.

Between eighteen months and thirty months of age, a child goes through a separation/individuation stage of development, leading to the beginnings of a unique and separate sense of self. Your Type's approach to independence and connection shapes how this vital process unfolds. See two-year-old Marcus asserting his growing independence with emphatic declarations of "No!" while still needing the secure base of his mother Lisa's (8) presence. Her Type Eight comfort with assertion creates an environment where his emerging autonomy can flourish.

From this point until around six, the child's world is primarily the family ecosystem that parents create through their Type's patterns. We can observe Sofia, age four, absorbing not just her mother Ana's (2) words but her entire Type Two way of being, learning patterns of relating that will shape her future connections. Ana focuses on relationships and helping create an environment where Sofia develops sophisticated emotional attunement.

From birth to six years of age, your Type patterns and interactions with your child influence their survival strategy, resulting in their emerging personality patterning. The primary emotions of your Enneagram triad—anger, fear, or shame—create the emotional landscape in which your child learns to navigate their feelings. At around six, the foundation of ego development completes with the formation and activation of the superego complex. From then on, your child lives in a world of dual inputs and mirroring—the external ecosystem you create and the internalized scrutiny and directives of the inner critic they've developed from absorbing your patterns.

Two Critical Phases

In this book, we focus specifically on the first six years, which are divided into two crucial phases where your Type's patterns profoundly influence your child's development.

The Foundation Years (0-3)

During these vital early years, your Type patterns lay down the initial structures of your child's personality and ego, creating the basic scaffolding of selfhood. Watch how Lucas, at eighteen months, develops fundamental attachment patterns through daily interactions with his mother, Rachel (3). Her Type Three focus on achievement and image creates an environment where he begins to associate success with connection. The neural pathways shaping future emotional responses form through every interaction with your Type-specific approach.

These years establish:

- Basic trust and security through your Type's approach to protection
- Primary attachment patterns based on your style of connection
- Early emotional regulation shaped by your emotional responses
- Fundamental response styles mirroring your Type's strategies
- Core relationship blueprints reflecting your patterns

Your presence and attunement during these years—filtered through your Type's particular focus—shape your child's developing nervous system reactions and patterns of perception. Notice how Emma's confident exploration at age two reflects Sarah's (1) consistent, supportive presence, even as she works with her Type One tendency toward perfectionism. Sarah's conscious engagement with her pattern creates space for Emma's authentic development.

The Patterning Years (3-6)

During this phase, the foundational elements organize into more recognizable personality patterns as your child adapts to your Type's characteristic approach. We start to see the emergence of more complex social behaviors, a stronger sense of "I," and the beginning of conscious strategy formation in relating to others, all shaped by your Type's particular ways of being in the world.

Watch Maya at age four:

- Testing different approaches to peer interaction that mirror Priya's (5) strategies
- Developing preferred response patterns that adapt to her environment
- Building on early attachment foundations formed with her parents

- Creating unique coping strategies influenced by her family ecosystem

Your child begins to experiment with different ways of being in the world, trying various relational strategies and developing preferences for specific approaches over others. These emerging patterns reflect sophisticated adaptations to your Type's focus, fears, and desires. However, these patterns are still fluid and more susceptible to your conscious work with your patterns than they will be in the future.

The Practice of Presence

This book invites you to relate to your child as a mystery emerging while working consciously with your Type's patterns. It asks you to hold your expectations—shaped by your Type's particular focus—lightly, so lightly they are transparent, allowing you to see the extraordinary being before you with fresh eyes. Watch how Marcus's mother, Lisa (8), learns to balance her Type Eight protective instincts with the space needed for his unique unfolding.

During these formative years, it is vital to cultivate a comfort with not-knowing—a particular challenge for your Type's characteristic approach to certainty and control. From the perspective of the Enneagram, we see young children as embodying "all types," representing the unity of the circle and the profound mystery of the emptiness within. They are not yet fixed in their patterns but remain fluid, dynamic, and full of potential.

The Necessity of Ego Development

The ego is not a thing, but a process.
It is the result of the body trying to maintain balance
amid the chaos of life.
Alan Watts

Ego development, along with the emergence of personality, is not something to fear or prevent; it is a necessary stage of human development. Sigmund Freud provided a crucial insight that remains relevant today: The ego is fundamentally a coping mechanism, developing to help us manage the complex demands of life.

Watch four-year-old Sofia navigate a playground conflict. When another child takes her favorite swing, she doesn't just react instinctively; she employs a complex strategy involving verbal negotiation, emotional appeal, and social awareness. This isn't manipulation; it's her developing ego at work, helping her balance her desires with social reality. Her strategies reflect adaptations to her mother Ana's (2) helping pattern and her father Carlos's (4) emotional intensity. Ana might worry about Sofia's assertiveness, but children need this healthy ego development.

This perspective transforms how we view our children's behaviors and patterns. What we might label as "difficult" behaviors are often ingenious coping strategies—our child's best attempt to meet their needs and handle the complexities of their experience while adapting to the demands of the external world, particularly the family ecosystem that our Type patterns create.

Consider these examples:

- Marcus's strong boundary-setting, adapting to Lisa's (8) patterns of protection and power
- Emma's careful rule-following, mirroring Sarah's (1) approach to order and correctness
- Maya's thoughtful observation, reflecting Priya's (5) tendencies toward analysis and distance
- Lucas's achievement focus, adapting to Rachel's (3) patterns of success and image

As Freud recognized, the ego develops as a mediator between our internal drives and the demands of external reality. Children experience this mediation process unfolding in real time as they adapt to the reality created by the focus, fears, and desires of the Types of their parents. We all have an ego structure and can do nothing to prevent its formation. It's essential in this dimension of experience.

The Unique Cognitive Landscape of Early Childhood

A child between birth and six possesses a cognitive architecture fundamentally different from older children and adults. While they may not yet have developed advanced abstract thought or mature logical reasoning, they possess remarkable cognitive abilities that manifest in various ways appropriate to their developmental stage.

Rapid Language Acquisition: Learning words means absorbing the entire emotional and cultural context of communication. Three-year-old Emma isn't simply memorizing vocabulary when she picks up her mother Sarah's (1) precise way of describing things; she's internalizing Sarah's Type One relationship with language—

the careful definitions, the need for exactness, and the implicit judgment about "right" and "wrong" ways of speaking.

Basic Cause-and-Effect Understanding: This first develops through direct physical experience and then expands into more complex emotional and social realms. Observe Marcus at two experimenting with dropping objects from different heights, pushing boundaries with his mother Lisa (8) and testing various emotional responses to similar situations. Each exploration builds his understanding of how the world works while adapting to Lisa's Type Eight comfort with impact and power.

Sophisticated Symbolic Play: Through play, children process complex emotional experiences and try different ways of being in the world. Maya's elaborate pretend scenarios aren't just entertainment; they're a sophisticated laboratory for understanding human relationships and developing emotional intelligence, even as they reflect adaptations to her mother Priya's (5) Type Five approach to engagement and distance.

Integrated Sensory and Motor Learning: Children at this age learn through their whole bodies. When Sofia explores her environment through movement, touch, and sensory investigation, these aren't just physical activities; they're the foundation for cognitive development, emotional regulation, and social understanding. Her explorations adapt to her father Carlos's (4) Type Four appreciation for aesthetic experience and emotional depth.

Nascent Emotional Intelligence: Young children are exquisitely attuned to emotional nuance, even before they have words to describe what they're sensing. Watch Lucas read his mother Rachel's (3) facial expressions, tone of voice, and body language with remarkable accuracy, absorbing not just what she says but also the Type Three emphasis on appearance, achievement, and the importance of how others perceive you.

Young children inhabit an intensely emotional and energetic world, experiencing life through immediate sensations, relationships, and direct experiences. Their cognitive processing is immediate, intuitive, and sensation-based—a radical departure from the analytical thinking of older children and adults. This makes them extraordinarily sensitive to the particular emotional atmosphere created by your Type patterns.

The Parent-Child Dance

Children are extraordinary mirrors, reflecting our deepest Type patterns, unresolved wounds, and hidden potentials. They invite us into a deeper understanding of ourselves, not through analysis but through direct experience of our patterns in action. Each interaction becomes a portal for mutual discovery.

Watch these mirroring moments unfold:

- Sarah (1) feels her perfectionism activate as Emma struggles with a drawing. Her immediate impulse to correct and improve reveals her Type One pattern and childhood experiences of never feeling "good enough." This awareness creates an opportunity: Can she support Emma's natural process without imposing her Type One standards?
- Lisa (8) notices her protective intensity rise when Marcus faces playground challenges. Her Type Eight pattern urges her to step in and show strength, but this reaction speaks to her own early experiences of vulnerability. Understanding this helps her balance protection with allowing Marcus to develop his resilience.
- Priya (5) recognizes her withdrawal impulse when Maya becomes emotionally expressive. Her Type Five pattern of creating distance reflects her childhood experiences of feeling overwhelmed. This recognition lets her stay present with Maya's feelings while managing her energy.

As parents, we often discover that our strongest reactions to our children's behaviors are windows into our Type's unresolved experiences:

- The child who constantly tests boundaries might trigger our Type's particular relationship with authority
- Our frustration with a slow-moving child might reveal our Type's uncomfortable relationship with time and productivity
- Our anxiety about a shy child might connect to our Type's early experiences of social insecurity

This mirroring effect offers an unprecedented opportunity for healing and growth. When you feel triggered by your child's behavior, you can ask yourself:

- What aspect of my Type pattern is being activated?
- What did I need in similar situations that I didn't receive?
- How can I provide for my child what I wished for myself?
- What would it mean to respond from presence rather than pattern?

This journey of self-discovery runs parallel to our child's development. As you become more aware of your Type patterns and projections, you create more space for your child's authentic unfolding. Consider these reflective questions:

- What aspects of my Type am I unconsciously transmitting?
- How do my Type's unresolved experiences shape my child's environment?
- Can I create space for my child's unique unfolding beyond my Type's focus?
- What expectations might I be holding that limit my child's potential?

This Book's Transformative Intent

This book supports child and parent development through conscious engagement with your Type patterns and how they shape your child's emerging personality. Watch how different Types create unique developmental environments:

Type Three Parent (Rachel) with Lucas:

- Building resilience beyond performance-based worth
- Finding flexibility in achievement orientation
- Developing healthy responses to success and failure
- Working with Type Three expectations around image

Type One Parent (Sarah) with Emma:

- Supporting natural development beyond perfectionism
- Creating space for "imperfect" exploration
- Working with Type One standards and criticism
- Building confidence through unconditional acceptance

Type Five Parent (Priya) with Maya:

- Maintaining connection despite withdrawal tendencies
- Supporting both retreat and engagement needs
- Finding rhythm between Type Five distance and presence
- Building trust through consistent availability

The book also helps you recognize and work with your Type's influence on your child's emerging patterns. For example, you might notice:

- Your naturally expressive child beginning to withdraw after repeatedly encountering your Type Five, Six, or Nine patterns around energy and emotion
- A typically cautious child becoming more adventurous when met with patient encouragement rather than your Type's particular anxiety
- An achievement-oriented child rediscovering joy in the process when your Type Three or One performance pressure eases

These emerging patterns don't define your child, but they offer important clues about how they're adapting to the environment created by your Type. You might see early signs of:

- How your child approaches challenges (adapting to your Type's relationship with difficulty)
- Their natural rhythm of engagement with others (mirroring your Type's connection style)
- Their response to sensory stimulation (influenced by your Type's comfort with intensity)
- Their way of processing emotions (reflecting your Type's emotional patterns)

Remember, these patterns are not fixed destinies but early adaptations to your Type's particular focus. They can become more rigid or remain flexible depending on how consciously you work with your patterns.

Attention is the rarest and purest form of generosity.

Simone Weil

This book offers a transformative practice that we'll explore through our journey:

- Moving from controlling to witnessing, as Lisa (8) learns to work with her Type Eight patterns

- Shifting from expectation to wonder, as Rachel (3) discovers flexibility in her Type Three focus
- Transforming judgment into curiosity, as Sarah (1) practices with her Type One inner critic
- Cultivating spacious, non-reactive presence, as Priya (5) develops beyond her Type Five withdrawal

Through understanding how your Type patterns influence your child's development, you develop:

- Deeper appreciation for your child's unique ways of being beyond your Type's focus
- Greater compassion for your Type patterns and history
- Richer awareness of how your Type shapes the parent-child dance
- More spacious presence in daily interactions

We are not human beings having a spiritual experience;
we are spiritual beings having a human experience.
Pierre Teilhard de Chardin

This book is a love letter to the mystery of human becoming. It invites you to let go of your Type's characteristic expectations, embrace the unknown beyond your Type's need for certainty, and discover the profound intelligence that emerges when you genuinely see beyond your Type's particular focus. Your child is not a project to be completed or a problem to be solved but a miracle to be appreciated—a unique expression of life unfolding before your eyes.

Watch the sacred unfolding as both your child and you transform:

- Emma discovering her voice beyond Sarah's Type One perfectionism
- Marcus exploring strength with sensitivity beyond Lisa's Type Eight intensity
- Maya finding her rhythm of engagement beyond Priya's Type Five withdrawal

- Sofia expressing her authentic nature beyond Ana's Type Two helping
- Lucas learning joy beyond Rachel's Type Three achievement focus

In this journey of mutual revelation, both parent and child are transformed. As you learn to hold your child's emerging self with an open heart that transcends your Type's particular focus, you create a container of love that allows their unique essence to flourish. And in that sacred space of witnessing you, too, are changed, growing into a more spacious and compassionate version of yourself beyond your Type's limitations.

As we begin exploring how personality patterns emerge and develop, we must first understand the fundamental need that shapes all aspects of early development—acceptance. In Chapter 1, we'll examine how your Type's approach to acceptance influences every aspect of your child's development, creating the ground from which all patterns grow.

Your Notes

Chapter 1

The Primal Need for Acceptance

When a flower doesn't bloom, you fix the environment in which it grows, not the flower.
Alexander Den Heijer

As we explore acceptance, we'll discover how this fundamental need shapes personality development and how different parents' patterns influence their children's experience of being accepted. We'll see how early experiences with acceptance create the foundation from which all other patterns grow.

Observe five-year-old Emma erasing her drawing for the third time. Her mother Sarah (1) feels her heart tighten as she recognizes the signs of perfectionism emerging. This isn't just about art; it's about Emma's developing sense that certain parts of her experience aren't acceptable. Each erasure raises a more profound question: "Will I be accepted as I am?"

At its most fundamental level, acceptance is simply openness to what is. This radically differs from approval or agreement. It is the capacity to remain present with reality as it unfolds without pushing away or grasping. When we truly accept, we create space to experience what arises in the moment, allowing us to respond with presence rather than react from our patterns.

Consider these contrasting moments:

> Maya discovers a caterpillar in the garden. Her natural response is complete absorption in observation. Priya's (5) pattern urges intellectual distance, but today, she chooses presence over teaching, creating space for Maya's authentic exploration.
>
> Marcus expresses intense anger at a friend: Raw emotional energy emerges. Lisa's (8) pattern appreciates the force, yet she maintains a containing presence that supports healthy expression without overwhelming.

Sofia expresses her feelings about a minor event: Emotional intensity flows naturally. Ana's (2) pattern wants to soothe and fix. Instead, she practices simple witnessing, allowing authentic emotional expression.

This distinction is crucial for understanding our children's development and our parenting patterns. Acceptance doesn't mean we approve of every behavior or circumstance. Instead, it means we maintain an open, receptive stance that allows us to:

- See clearly what is happening
- Stay present with our reactions and emotions
- Respond from wisdom rather than conditioning
- Hold space for authentic expression and growth

Understanding how children experience and adapt to their parents' understanding of acceptance gives us unprecedented opportunities to support healthy development while maintaining flexibility in these vital patterns.

The Nature of Acceptance

Watch how different parent patterns create distinct acceptance environments for their children.

Body Center Patterns

Type Eight Parents (Like Lisa)

When Marcus shows vulnerability, Lisa's pattern influences his experience of acceptance.

Without awareness, she might:

- Push for strength over sensitivity
- Dismiss softer emotions
- Overemphasize protection
- Create pressure for toughness

Through conscious work, she learns to:

- Accept vulnerability alongside strength
- Welcome all emotional expressions
- Balance protection with tenderness
- Create space for gentleness

Daily life reveals this transformation when Marcus cries after falling. Instead of quickly encouraging toughness, Lisa stays present with his experience, teaching that strength and sensitivity are acceptable.

Type Nine Parents (Like David)

When children express strong opinions, David's pattern shapes their experience.

Without awareness, he might:

- Minimize differences to maintain peace
- Absorb others' desires over his own
- Avoid acknowledging conflict
- Create pressure for harmony

Through conscious work, he learns to:

- Accept disagreement alongside agreement
- Welcome passionate expression
- Balance peace with authentic difference
- Create space for healthy conflict

Daily life shows this growth when Marcus expresses a strong opinion contrary to David's. Instead of merging or withdrawing, David stays present with the discomfort, showing that differences don't threaten connection.

Type One Parents (Like Sarah)

Watch Sarah's pattern shape Emma's understanding of acceptance.

Without awareness, she might:

- Focus on improvement
- Notice imperfections
- Correct natural expression
- Create standards for acceptance

Through development, she learns to:

- Accept what is while supporting growth
- Welcome messy exploration
- Allow natural development
- Create space for imperfection

Daily moments reveal this transformation when Emma's art project doesn't match Sarah's vision. Instead of suggesting improvements, Sarah appreciates Emma's creative process, teaching that expression doesn't need to be perfect to be valued.

Heart Center Patterns

Type Two Parents (Like Ana)

Sofia experiences acceptance through her mother's helping pattern.

Without awareness, Ana might:

- Make acceptance conditional on connection
- Over-focus on others' needs
- Miss independent exploration
- Create pressure for attunement

Through conscious work, she learns to:

- Accept separation alongside connection
- Welcome autonomous exploration
- Balance helping with space
- Create room for independence

Daily moments reveal this growth when Sofia wants to play alone. Instead of feeling rejected, Ana practices accepting this natural need for space.

Type Three Parents (Like Rachel)

Lucas encounters acceptance through his mother's achievement lens.

Without awareness, Rachel might:

- Link acceptance to performance
- Focus on successful outcomes
- Miss process exploration
- Create pressure for achievement

Through development, she learns to:

- Accept being alongside doing
- Welcome natural rhythm
- Balance achievement with presence
- Create space for authentic expression

Daily life shows this when Lucas becomes absorbed in building without completing any structure. Instead of redirecting toward a finished product, Rachel joins his exploration, teaching that the process has value beyond outcomes.

Type Four Parents (Like Carlos)

Sofia experiences acceptance through her father's uniqueness pattern.

Without awareness, Carlos might:

- Emphasize emotional depth over simplicity
- Focus on special qualities
- Miss ordinary joy
- Create pressure for significance

Through conscious work, he learns to:

- Accept ordinary alongside extraordinary
- Welcome simple happiness
- Balance depth with lightness
- Create space for everyday experience

Daily life demonstrates this when Sofia shares a simple pleasure. Instead of intensifying or complicating the moment, Carlos stays present with its simple joy, showing that ordinary experiences are also worthy of celebration.

Head Center Patterns

Type Five Parents (Like Priya)

Maya experiences acceptance through her mother's observant pattern.

Without awareness, Priya might:

- Create distance for comfort
- Focus on understanding over feeling
- Miss emotional connection
- Build walls of knowledge

Through conscious work, she learns to:

- Accept engagement alongside observation
- Welcome emotional expression
- Balance understanding with presence
- Create space for connection

Watch this transform when Maya expresses intense excitement. Instead of withdrawing, Priya stays present with the energy, showing that all levels of expression are acceptable.

Type Six Parents (Like Michael)

Emma encounters acceptance through her father's vigilant pattern.

Without awareness, Michael might:

- Focus on potential problems
- Express doubt about capabilities
- Overemphasize preparation
- Create pressure for caution

Through development, he learns to:

- Accept uncertainty alongside readiness
- Welcome brave exploration
- Balance preparation with trust
- Create space for confidence

Daily moments reveal this when Emma ventures to climb higher at the playground. Instead of warning of dangers, Michael stays present with his anxiety while supporting her exploration, teaching that both caution and courage have their place.

Type Seven Parents

Maya experiences acceptance through her father's enthusiastic pattern.

Without awareness, a Type Seven parent like Raj might:

- Redirect from difficult emotions
- Focus on positive experiences
- Miss opportunities for depth
- Create pressure for happiness

Through conscious work, he learns to:

- Accept difficulty alongside joy
- Welcome full emotional range
- Balance positivity with depth
- Create space for necessary pain

Daily life shows this transformation when Maya expresses sadness or frustration. Instead of quickly cheering her up or distracting her, Raj stays present with the discomfort, demonstrating that all emotions are acceptable parts of being human.

How you work with your Type's patterns shapes how your child experiences acceptance. This isn't about perfect acceptance but developing enough flexibility that your child can feel genuinely seen and accepted while you maintain healthy boundaries and growth.

The Impact of Acceptance on Personality Development

The Enneagram reveals how children develop strategies to secure acceptance based on their family environment. Watch how these patterns emerge and solidify.

Early Formation (0-2 years)

Emma experiences her mother Sarah's (1) pattern through:

- Physical tension during feeding
- Reactions to messiness
- Responses to exploration
- Handling of mistakes

Infants absorb basic emotional tones, sensing the underlying atmosphere of their environment:

- Core messages about what's acceptable
- Basic patterns of approval and disapproval
- Fundamental experiences of being received
- Early lessons about conditional acceptance

Watch this early patterning:

- Sarah's slight body tension when Emma spills
- The unconscious sigh at disordered play
- Quick movements to "fix" situations
- Subtle praise for "correct" behavior

Pattern Development (2-4 years)

Marcus begins actively incorporating his parents' patterns through:

- Lisa's (8) direct modeling of strength
- David's (9) peace-seeking responses
- Their combined messages about power and harmony
- Complex expectations around assertion

Marcus develops initial self-talk about strength:

- "I'm strong!" becoming a frequent affirmation
- Quick recovery from falls emphasized
- Protection of smaller children praised
- Resistance to showing hurt reinforced

Marcus's adaptation to his parents' patterns reveals itself in daily life through his enthusiastic declarations of power and strength, his natural emergence as a protector of others, his determined and persistent responses to challenges, and his complex developing relationship with vulnerability and tenderness.

Pattern Consolidation (4-6 years)

Sofia solidifies her acceptance strategy, influenced by both Ana's (2) and Carlos's (4) patterns:

- Complex role modeling around helping and uniqueness
- Explicit expectations about emotional sensitivity
- Social comparisons about significance
- Performance feedback about specialness

She establishes:

- Consistent ways of seeking acceptance
- Fixed patterns of securing connection
- Stable strategies for maintaining worth
- Regular methods of ensuring recognition

Watch different children adapt their strategies:

Maya with Priya (5)

Learns that acceptance comes through:

- Careful observation
- Thoughtful responses
- Managed energy
- Controlled engagement

Lucas with Rachel (3)

Develops understanding that acceptance requires:

- Successful performance

- Visible achievement
- Image management
- Constant improvement

Emma with Sarah (1)

Forms belief that acceptance depends on:

- Meeting standards
- Following rules
- Showing improvement
- Maintaining order

These patterns become established through daily interactions, gradually shaping how children understand what makes them acceptable and lovable. Without parents' conscious awareness, these early adaptations can become rigid strategies for securing acceptance.

Supporting Development through Acceptance

Understanding how acceptance patterns transmit transforms how we approach supporting children's development. Our role is to recognize our barriers to openness while creating an ecosystem where authentic expression can flourish. By working with our Type-specific patterns around acceptance, we develop greater capacity to be present with what is, allowing us and our children to grow in an atmosphere of genuine recognition.

Working with Different Parent Patterns

The Connor Family Ecosystem

Sarah (1) and Michael (6) create an environment where:

- Perfectionism becomes a shield against rejection
- Mistakes carry heavy emotional weight
- Security comes through correctness

- Worth is tied to being "good"

Through conscious work, Sarah and Michael learn to accept natural exploration without imposing structure or safety measures, support messy discovery rather than insisting on order and predictability, allow authentic expression without correction or improvement, and maintain loving presence that isn't contingent on meeting their standards or expectations.

The Patel Family System

Priya (5) and Raj (7) establish an environment where:

- Knowledge provides safety
- Understanding creates acceptance
- Distance manages connection
- Options maintain security

Priya and Raj's growth involves learning to accept emotional expression without withdrawal or deflection, supporting energetic engagement despite their tendencies toward conservation and avoidance, allowing natural intensity rather than dampening or redirecting it, and maintaining a steady presence when their patterns urge retreat or movement.

Supporting Different Response Patterns

The Performance-sensitive Child

When Lucas feels uncertain about acceptance, Rachel (3) learns to:

Provide Immediate Support:

- Maintain steady presence
- Allow natural processing
- Offer simple acknowledgment
- Create space for recovery

Develop Long-term Strategies:

- Support worth beyond achievement
- Build genuine self-acceptance
- Create safety for mistakes
- Maintain unconditional connection

The Connection-sensitive Child

When Sofia seeks acceptance through helping, Ana (2) practices:

Immediate Response:

- Stay present without fixing
- Allow natural emotional flow
- Support without overwhelming
- Maintain gentle presence

Long-term Development:

- Build healthy boundaries
- Support authentic needs
- Create balanced helping
- Maintain self-connection

Integration in Daily Life

Watch how different families navigate acceptance.

The Connor Family with Emma:

- Creating space for imperfection
- Supporting natural rhythm
- Allowing messy process
- Maintaining loving presence

The Patel Family with Maya:

- Respecting observation needs
- Supporting gradual engagement
- Allowing natural withdrawal
- Maintaining steady connection

The goal isn't to achieve acceptance but to remain open to your child's authentic experience in the moment. Acceptance isn't about approval or disapproval but creating space where your child's essence can be recognized without rejection. By understanding that acceptance means being present with what is, including your child's experience and your reactions to it, you create an environment where patterns can remain flexible rather than rigid. This deeper, more nuanced understanding allows you to explore your child's authentic unfolding and your Type-specific barriers to openness, creating conditions for genuine connection beyond judgment.

True integration happens when families can:

- Experience acceptance without conditions
- Maintain connection through difficulty
- Recover naturally from ruptures
- Access multiple ways of being present

This pattern develops through daily emotional attunement, where parents learn to:

- Read and respond to their child's cues
- Establish clear but kind boundaries
- Create predictable responses
- Maintain flexibility for authentic expression

As we move from exploring acceptance to examining attachment, remember that your Type's patterns fundamentally shape these vital processes. Your particular approach to acceptance—filtered through your Type's lens—lays the groundwork for how you create attachment with your child. In the next chapter, we'll discover how your way of connecting and separating influences your child's developing sense of security and exploration. We'll see how the foundation of acceptance you provide shapes the web of connection that your child weaves with you and eventually with others.

Reflection

Take a few quiet moments to explore your relationship with acceptance—how you experienced it in childhood and how your Type influences your capacity to offer it as a parent.

Your Pattern's Influence

Consider your automatic responses.

- What aspects of your child do you struggle to accept?
- How does your Type typically manage acceptance?
- Where do you feel most challenged?
- What helps you stay open and receptive?

The Living Laboratory

Consider a recent moment of challenge.

- What happened in your body?
- How did your pattern want to respond?
- Where did you find flexibility?
- What helped you maintain acceptance?

Remember: Acceptance doesn't mean approving of everything but maintaining an open, receptive stance that allows authentic development to unfold.

Your Notes

Chapter 2

The Web of Connection

The quality of our early bonds shapes the lens through which we view all future relationships.
John Bowlby

As we explore attachment, we'll discover how this vital process shapes personality development and how different parent patterns influence their children's experience of connection. We'll see how early experiences with acceptance lay the foundation for attachment patterns that affect all future relationships.

Three-year-old Emma falls while running in the park. For a moment, she lies still, then lifts her head to look for her mother Sarah (1). In that split second, before she reacts, she's asking an unconscious but profound question: "Are you there for me?" Sarah feels her pattern activate—the urge to quickly correct Emma's "careless" running. But today, something different happens. She notices her pattern, takes a breath, and moves closer, allowing Emma to guide her response to this moment.

This scene—repeated in countless variations throughout early childhood—illuminates how attachment patterns form. Observe, and you'll see three essential dynamics at play:

- The child's natural movement between exploration and connection
- The parent's capacity for attunement and response
- The dance of repair when inevitable ruptures occur

Watch how different parent patterns influence this fundamental process:

- Maya, at nine months, crawls away from Priya (5) to examine a toy, then turns back to check her presence. This isn't indecision; it's the development of secure attachment. She's learning she can explore while maintaining connection. Priya, working with her Type Five tendencies, practices staying visible and available even when her pattern urges withdrawal.

- Marcus at two, emphatically declares "No!" to sharing. His mother Lisa (8) feels her pattern appreciating his strength, while his father David (9) tenses at the potential conflict. Their contrasting responses create the ecosystem where Marcus learns to navigate his needs for both assertion and connection.
- Sofia at four, processes complex feelings about a friend moving away. Ana (2) notices her helping pattern activate—the urge to quickly soothe and fix. Instead, she practices staying present with Sofia's emotions, allowing her daughter to develop her relationship with loss and connection.

Understanding how children adapt to their parents' attachment patterns gives us unprecedented opportunities to support healthy development while maintaining flexibility in these vital patterns. Our role isn't to achieve perfect attachment—that's neither possible nor desirable—but to provide "good enough" connection while working consciously with our patterns.

The Nature of Attachment

When two-year-old Marcus protests his mother Lisa's (8) departure at preschool, he's not being difficult or manipulative. He's engaged in the essential work of understanding whether his world is fundamentally reliable, whether his needs matter, and whether he can trust in emotional connection. Building on the foundation of acceptance we explored in Chapter 1, attachment adds another crucial layer: the active dance of connection, separation, and reunion that shapes all future relationships.

Head Center Patterns

Type Five Parents (Like Priya)

Watch how Priya's pattern influences Maya's attachment formation.

Without awareness, she might:

- Create emotional distance for comfort
- Withdraw when feeling overwhelmed
- Prioritize understanding over connection
- Miss opportunities for emotional bonding

Through conscious work, she learns to:

- Stay present despite discomfort
- Maintain connection while managing energy
- Balance observation with engagement
- Create reliable emotional availability

Maya's daily life reveals this when she reaches for connection. Instead of automatically stepping back, Priya practices staying engaged while honoring her need for space.

Type Six Parents (Like Michael)

Observe how Michael's pattern shapes Emma's attachment experience.

Without awareness, he might:

- Transmit anxiety about separation
- Create hypervigilance around safety
- Miss opportunities for confidence-building
- Struggle with allowing healthy risk

Through development, he learns to:

- Contain his anxiety without passing it on
- Support brave exploration despite fears
- Balance caution with encouragement
- Create secure but flexible boundaries

Daily interactions reveal this growth when Emma ventures further at the playground. Michael notices his worry rising but stays present without warnings, allowing her to develop confidence through supported exploration.

Type Seven Parents

Watch how a Type Seven parent like Raj influences attachment formation.

Without awareness, he might:

- Create unpredictable engagement patterns
- Move quickly from one activity to another
- Miss opportunities for sustained connection
- Struggle with emotional depth

Through conscious work, he learns to:

- Maintain consistent presence
- Stay with one interaction longer
- Balance fun with emotional depth
- Create reliable but joyful connection

Daily moments show this transformation when Maya shares difficult feelings and, instead of brightening the mood, Raj stays present with the discomfort, building trust in his availability through all emotional states.

Heart Center Patterns

Type Two Parents (Like Ana)

Observe how Ana's pattern shapes Sofia's attachment experience.

Without awareness, she might:

- Over-attune to every need
- Create dependency through helping
- Miss opportunities for independence
- Struggle with healthy separation

Through development, she learns to:

- Allow natural independence
- Support autonomous exploration
- Maintain balanced connection
- Create space for separation

Sofia's daily life shows this growth when she ventures to play alone. Instead of following to help, Ana stays available but separate, allowing Sofia to develop confidence in both connection and autonomy.

Type Three Parents (Like Rachel)

Watch how Rachel's pattern influences Lucas's attachment.

Without awareness, she might:

- Link connection to performance
- Create conditional availability
- Miss opportunities for simply being together
- Struggle with unproductive time

Through conscious work, she learns to:

- Maintain presence without agenda
- Support connection beyond achievement
- Balance doing with being
- Create space for unstructured togetherness

Lucas's daily moments reveal this when he wants to sit together without activity. Rachel practices staying present without suggesting goals or improvements, building his trust that connection isn't tied to performance.

Type Four Parents

Observe how a Type Four parent like Carlos shapes attachment.

Without awareness, he might:

- Create emotional intensity in connection
- Focus on special, meaningful moments
- Miss opportunities for ordinary togetherness
- Struggle with consistent availability

Through development, he learns to:

- Moderate emotional intensity
- Find value in everyday connection
- Balance depth with consistency
- Create reliable emotional presence

Daily interactions show this growth when Sofia seeks ordinary help. Instead of making the moment special or significant, Carlos responds with simple presence, teaching that connection happens in profound and mundane moments.

Body Center Patterns

Type Eight Parents (Like Lisa)

Watch how Lisa's pattern influences Marcus's attachment.

Without awareness, she might:

- Push for independence too quickly
- Miss subtle connection needs
- Overwhelm with intensity
- Create pressure for strength

Through conscious work, she learns to:

- Balance protection with tenderness
- Support gentle connection
- Allow vulnerability
- Create emotional safety

Marcus's daily life reveals this when he reaches for comfort after falling. Instead of quickly encouraging toughness, Lisa holds space for his vulnerability, building trust that both strength and softness are welcome.

Type Nine Parents (Like David)

Observe how David's pattern shapes attachment formation.

Without awareness, he might:

- Merge with the child's needs
- Create unclear boundaries
- Miss opportunities for healthy differentiation
- Struggle with consistent engagement

Through development, he learns to:

- Maintain his presence
- Support clear but loving boundaries
- Balance merging with separateness
- Create reliable but peaceful connection

Daily moments show this transformation when Marcus tests boundaries. Instead of accommodating or withdrawing, David stays engaged with the discomfort while maintaining clear limits, teaching that connection remains through disagreement.

Type One Parents (Like Sarah)

Watch how a Type One parent like Sarah influences attachment.

Without awareness, she might:

- Create structured connection times
- Focus on proper relationship behavior
- Miss spontaneous connection opportunities
- Struggle with messy emotional expression

Through conscious work, she learns to:

- Allow connection outside of structure
- Support imperfect emotional expression
- Balance clarity with flexibility
- Create space for authentic relating

Emma's daily life reveals this when she seeks connection at inconvenient times. Sarah practices responding to these bids despite her schedule, building Emma's trust that relationship isn't contingent on doing things "right."

Each Type's pattern creates a distinct attachment environment, shaping how children learn to connect, separate, and return. By understanding your specific patterns, you can work more consciously with attachment, supporting your child's developing sense of security while maintaining enough flexibility for authentic connection to flourish.

The Patterning Years (3-6): Expanding the Web

Attachment expands beyond the primary caregiver relationship as children enter the patterning years. Watch how early attachment patterns influence broader social engagement.

Complex Social Relationships (3-4 years)

Emma in Preschool

Building on her secure base with Sarah (1):

- Forms friendships while maintaining connection
- Navigates peer conflicts with growing confidence
- Expresses emotions within relationships
- Uses teacher relationships as secure extensions

Sarah supports her child's expanding world by:

- Maintaining steady, grounding presence through transitions
- Working with her Type One tendency to control or correct
- Creating space for emotional processing
- Supporting social exploration without excessive structuring

Marcus at Play

Extending his connection with Lisa (8):

- Shows leadership in peer groups
- Protects younger children
- Navigates power dynamics
- Maintains emotional regulation

Lisa facilitates her child's development by:

- Supporting healthy assertion while tempering Type Eight intensity
- Finding ways to encourage strength without overwhelming
- Modeling balanced protection that respects boundaries
- Creating an environment where vulnerability can safely exist

Emotional Storytelling (4-5 years)

Sofia's Development

Growing from her bond with Ana (2):

- Creates rich emotional narratives
- Processes feelings through play
- Develops friendship stories
- Explores relationship dynamics

Ana supports her child's development by:

- Validating emotional expression without getting enmeshed
- Working with her Type Two tendency to merge or fix feelings
- Practicing allowing independent emotional processing
- Maintaining connected presence that supports without overwhelming

Maya's Journey

Building on Priya's (5) attunement:

- Develops observation skills
- Creates thoughtful connections
- Processes experiences quietly
- Forms selective friendships

Priya nurtures her child's development by:

- Respecting her need for processing time
- Supporting careful engagement while working with Type Five withdrawal
- Finding ways to maintain reliable presence despite energy depletion
- Allowing natural rhythm of connection and withdrawal

Integration of Attachment Patterns (5-6 years)

Lucas's Growth

Expanding from Rachel's (3) foundation:

- Balances achievement and connection
- Forms authentic friendships
- Navigates group dynamics
- Maintains emotional authenticity

Rachel supports her child's growth by:

- Consciously celebrating relationship over achievement
- Working against Type Three tendency to focus on doing
- Practicing validating emotional needs rather than solutions
- Maintaining presence not tied to performance

Marcus's Development

Building on Lisa's (8) groundwork:

- Combines strength with sensitivity
- Forms protective friendships
- Navigates power with care
- Maintains emotional connection

Through these stages, we see how children adapt to and integrate their parents' attachment patterns while developing unique ways of connecting. The goal isn't to achieve perfect attachment but to maintain enough flexibility to evolve these patterns throughout life.

Understanding Attachment through the Enneagram Lens

The Enneagram reveals nine ways parents naturally support or inadvertently complicate secure attachment. While we never type young children, understanding these patterns helps us recognize how our attachment history influences our parenting.

Working with Different Parent Patterns

Type Eight Parents (Lisa)

Watch Lisa with Marcus during a playground conflict. Instead of rushing to solve the problem, she moves closer, allowing him to handle it himself. Her strong presence provides a secure base, and this natural capacity for protective presence supports secure attachment.

Strengths:

- Clear boundaries
- Strong protection
- Direct engagement
- Reliable presence

Growth Edges:

- Allowing vulnerability
- Supporting soft emotions
- Maintaining gentle connection
- Moderating intensity

Lisa works with her Type Eight patterns by learning to notice protective impulses before they become overwhelming, catching herself when the instinct to shield or defend arises too strongly, finding ways to support emotional expression while maintaining strength, and creating space for both vulnerability and power in her parenting relationship.

Type Nine Parents (David)

Observe David sitting with Marcus through a tantrum, neither withdrawing nor forcing a resolution. This capacity for steady, accepting presence helps a child feel secure in all emotional states.

Strengths:

- Patient presence
- Calm acceptance
- Steady support
- Peaceful containment

Growth Edges:

- Maintaining boundaries
- Supporting assertion
- Staying engaged with conflict
- Expressing preferences

David develops in his parenting journey by recognizing when his Type Nine pattern leads to merging with his child's wants and needs at his own expense, maintaining healthy boundaries even when uncomfortable, supporting active engagement rather than defaulting to peace at any price, and expressing clear preferences and positions while maintaining loving connection.

Type One Parents (Sarah)
Consider Sarah creating predictable routines for Emma, which help her feel secure through reliable structure. Her natural appreciation for order supports attachment through dependability.

Strengths:

- Consistent structure
- Clear guidelines
- Reliable presence
- Stable environment

Growth Edges:

- Allowing messiness
- Supporting spontaneity
- Maintaining flexibility
- Accepting imperfection

Sarah grows through her parenting journey by learning to catch perfectionist impulses before they narrow her child's expression. She supports exploratory play without needing to structure or direct it, creates space for imperfection and organic growth, and maintains a loving presence that isn't contingent on correctness or achievement.

Heart Center Patterns

Type Two Parents (Ana)

Watch Ana give Sofia space to solve a friendship challenge. Instead of rushing to help or fix it, she maintains a supportive presence while allowing autonomy.

Strengths:

- Emotional attunement
- Nurturing presence
- Responsive care
- Empathic understanding

Growth Edges:

- Allowing independence
- Supporting separation
- Maintaining boundaries
- Respecting distance needs

Ana develops through her parenting journey by learning to recognize her helping impulses before they interfere with her child's natural independence, catching herself when she rushes to assist without being asked, supporting autonomous growth by stepping back when her pattern urges her to step in, and maintaining healthy emotional distance while allowing natural separation to unfold.

Type Three Parents (Rachel)

Observe Rachel sitting with Lucas through frustration with a difficult puzzle, focusing on his experience rather than the achievement outcome.

Strengths:

- Achievement support
- Confidence building
- Success focus
- Goal orientation

Growth Edges:

- Allowing process
- Supporting being over doing
- Maintaining unconditional connection
- Accepting non-achievement

Rachel grows in her parenting journey by learning to catch her Type Three performance focus before it shapes her child's experience, noticing when her attention automatically shifts to outcomes rather than process, practicing supporting simple presence even when nothing measurable is accomplished, and maintaining deep emotional bonds that aren't tied to performance or success.

Type Four Parents (Carlos)

Consider Carlos helping Sofia explore her complex feelings about a friend moving away, validating her unique emotional experience while helping her find her way through.

Strengths:

- Emotional depth
- Authentic expression
- Unique connection
- Intensity tolerance

Growth Edges:

- Supporting ordinary experience
- Containing emotional intensity
- Maintaining consistency
- Balancing depth with routine

Carlos develops in his parenting journey by recognizing his Type Four tendency to amplify emotional intensity, practicing supporting simple moments rather than seeking the extraordinary, maintaining emotional balance when his pattern urges heightened reactions, and celebrating ordinary connections and experiences with his child.

Head Center Patterns

Type Five Parents (Priya)

Watch Priya stay engaged with Maya during an exciting playground visit despite feeling energy depletion. She maintains connection while respecting her own boundaries.

Strengths:

- Respect for independence
- Knowledge sharing
- Space allowing
- Careful observation

Growth Edges:

- Maintaining connection
- Supporting needs
- Staying emotionally present
- Engaging with intensity

Priya develops in her parenting journey by learning to recognize her Type Five withdrawal impulses before they create emotional distance, catching herself when she begins to retreat into her mind rather than staying present, supporting emotional needs even when they feel overwhelming, and allowing a more energetic connection when her pattern urges observation from a distance.

Type Six Parents (Michael)

Observe Michael supporting Emma as she tries something challenging. He contains his anxiety while maintaining a secure presence that encourages healthy risk-taking.

Strengths:

- Safety awareness
- Consistent support
- Careful preparation
- Reliable presence

Growth Edges:

- Managing own anxiety
- Supporting risk-taking
- Maintaining confidence
- Allowing uncertainty

Michael grows in his parenting journey by learning to recognize his Type Six anxiety patterns before they limit his child's exploration, catching himself when fear of what might go wrong overshadows potential growth, supporting brave exploration even when his instinct is to warn or protect, and maintaining a steady presence that can hold both caution and adventure.

Type Seven Parents (Raj)

Watch a Type Seven parent like Raj staying present with Maya during a disappointing moment rather than immediately shifting to another activity or brightening the mood.

Strengths:

- Playful engagement
- Positive reframing
- Adventure creation
- Energy management

Growth Edges:

- Staying with difficult emotions
- Supporting processing
- Maintaining connection depth
- Allowing discomfort

Raj develops in his parenting journey by learning to recognize his Type Seven avoidance patterns before they deflect from deeper emotional experiences, catching himself when he automatically tries to lighten or redirect difficult moments, supporting emotional depth even when his instinct is to move toward pleasure, and maintaining present focus when his pattern urges him to jump to future possibilities.

Each Type brings unique gifts and challenges to the parenting journey. By understanding your specific pattern, you can work more consciously with your strengths while developing greater flexibility in your growth areas, creating an environment where you and your child can flourish.

Supporting Different Attachment Needs

The Proximity Seeker

Four-year-old Emma needs frequent physical connection to feel secure. She regularly returns to Sarah (1) for quick hugs during play—not because she's insecure, but because this pattern of connection and exploration works for her.

Supporting her means:

- Remaining physically accessible
- Welcoming brief check-ins
- Celebrating independence
- Maintaining emotional presence

Sarah works with her Type One pattern by learning to allow natural "interruptions" to her carefully planned activities. She recognizes that these moments of connection build security rather than create disorder.

The Independent Explorer

Six-year-old Marcus prefers to explore widely, checking back mainly through eye contact or quick glances. His attachment needs are as real as Emma's, but they express themselves differently.

Supporting him means:

- Staying visible and available
- Responding to subtle connection bids
- Maintaining emotional accessibility
- Respecting his space

Lisa (8) learns to work with her Type Eight energy by consciously moderating her natural intensity, finding ways to maintain a firm yet gentle presence that supports independent exploration.

The Emotional Processor

Five-year-old Sofia needs to talk through experiences to feel secure. Her constant narration isn't attention-seeking but her way of maintaining connection.

Supporting her means:

- Listening without fixing
- Validating emotional experiences
- Helping to name feelings
- Staying present for processing

Ana (2) works with her pattern by offering support without overwhelming, allowing space for independent processing, maintaining an appropriate distance, and providing a steady, reassuring presence.

The Cautious Observer

Maya takes time to warm up in new situations, carefully observing before engaging. Her methodical approach to connection isn't fear-based but her way of creating security.

Supporting her means:

- Allowing observation time
- Respecting her pace
- Creating predictable transitions
- Maintaining patient presence

Priya (5) works with her Type Five pattern by finding balance between honoring Maya's careful approach and gently supporting gradual engagement without imposing her preference for observation.

The Rhythm Keeper

Lucas develops security through predictable patterns of connection and separation. His attachment needs express through timing and routine rather than constant proximity.

Supporting him means:

- Maintaining consistent rhythms
- Providing clear transitions
- Creating reliable reunion rituals
- Honoring timing needs

Rachel (3) works with her Type Three pattern by finding value in these simple rhythms rather than seeing them as inefficient or unproductive. She learns that security often comes through predictability rather than achievement.

The Physical Connector

Some children, like Marcus, process attachment primarily through physical movement and sensory experience. Their bodies tell the story of their security.

Supporting them means:

- Providing physical play opportunities
- Engaging through movement
- Respecting sensory needs
- Creating physical containment

David (9) works with his Type Nine pattern by engaging more actively than might feel natural, finding ways to stay physically present when he tends to become passive or withdraw into mental activity.

The Social Bridger

Children like Sofia sometimes maintain attachment through triangulated connections, using friends, toys, or activities as bridges to their caregivers.

Supporting them means:

- Engaging with their interests
- Participating in their social world
- Creating shared activities

- Building connection through community

Carlos (4) works with his Type Four pattern by finding value in ordinary social connections rather than seeking only special or unique moments, recognizing that everyday bridges build security.

The Intensity Seeker

Some children require periods of deep, concentrated connection to feel secure. Their attachment needs come in waves of focused engagement followed by independence.

Supporting them means:

- Providing undivided attention periods
- Creating deep connection rituals
- Honoring the intensity cycle
- Fully engaging during connection times

Type Seven parents work with their pattern by staying fully present during these intense connection periods rather than dispersing energy or planning the next activity. They find value in the depth rather than breadth of experience.

The Parallel Player

Children like Maya sometimes maintain security through nearby but separate activities. Their attachment expresses through shared space rather than direct interaction.

Supporting them means:

- Maintaining proximity without intrusion
- Creating side-by-side activities
- Respecting personal space
- Offering occasional connection bids

Type Two parents work with their pattern by resisting the urge to create more active connection, recognizing that presence without helping or managing can be a profound form of support.

Understanding these patterns helps create secure foundations while maintaining flexibility for continued growth. The goal isn't perfect attachment but "good enough" connection that supports healthy development while allowing for natural variation in how children express and experience attachment needs.

Each child may show different tendencies in different contexts or developmental stages. By recognizing their unique attachment expression, you can work more consciously with your Type patterns to support their security while fostering healthy independence. Your awareness creates space for both of you to grow—your child in their authentic connection style and you in your flexibility to meet their needs beyond your Type's habitual approach.

Moving Forward

As we shift from examining attachment to exploring anger, consider how your Type's patterns for connection influence your approach to this vital emotion. Your characteristic way of handling attachment creates the context in which your child first experiences and expresses their life force. In the next chapter, we'll discover how your relationship with anger—shaped by your Type's particular focus—creates the environment in which your child learns to navigate their forceful energy and boundary-setting. We'll see how your established attachment patterns influence your child's developing relationship with this essential emotion.

Reflection

Take a few quiet moments to explore your relationship with attachment—both how you experienced it in childhood and how your Type influences your capacity for connection as a parent.

Your Pattern's Dance with Connection

Consider your automatic responses.

- What aspects of connection activate your pattern?
- How does your Type typically manage separation?
- Where do you feel most challenged by your child's attachment needs?
- What helps you stay present with connection?

The Living Laboratory

Think about a recent attachment moment with your child.

- What happened in your body?
- How did your pattern want to respond?
- Where did you find flexibility?
- What supported your ability to stay connected?

Remember: Secure attachment doesn't mean perfect connection but maintaining enough flexibility that both parent and child can explore while staying safely connected.

Your Notes

Chapter 3

The Primary Emotions

The parenting journey is one step toward them and one step toward yourself.

As we move from exploring attachment to exploring emotional development, we must understand a fundamental truth: **A young child is not primarily an intellectual being but an energetic, emotional one.**

Watch Maya at three, her whole body involved in protest, or Lucas at four, vibrating excitedly over a discovery. Their emotions aren't just feelings; they are full-bodied experiences that shape their entire way of being in the world.

> The Enneagram reveals three primary emotions—anger, fear, and shame—that form foundational building blocks of personality.

The Primary Emotions of Personality Development

These aren't just passing states but powerful forces that shape how children relate to themselves, others, and the world. Each emotion serves a vital developmental purpose:

- Anger energizes boundary-setting and self-assertion
- Fear guides protection and discernment

- Shame supports social learning and belonging

Anger and fear emerge from our most basic survival instinct—the fight-or-flight response that helps us navigate physical threats. These emotions are hardwired into our nervous system, providing essential information about safety and boundaries. However, as consciousness develops in early childhood, these survival emotions also become enlisted in psychological survival.

Shame enters the picture through our uniquely human capacity for self-reflection and social comparison. Unlike anger and fear, which we share with other animals, shame requires the cognitive ability to see ourselves as objects that can be evaluated and found wanting. This comparative mind creates a sense of deficiency that becomes endemic to ego development - the persistent feeling that we are somehow not enough as we are.

These three emotions become primary architects of personality because:

- Anger powers boundary formation and self-assertion
- Fear guides safety assessment and threat response
- Shame shapes social belonging and self-image

This emotional trinity forms the foundation from which distinct personality patterns emerge. What makes these three emotions so foundational is that each addresses a core aspect of existential continuity—the fundamental need to secure one's ongoing existence and coherence in the world. Anger establishes boundaries that affirm "I am here and matter"; fear creates safety maps that ensure "I can navigate and survive"; shame develops social attunement that maintains "I belong and have value." Each Enneagram type represents a unique strategy for managing these existential concerns—a characteristic response to perceived threats to continuity.

We can observe these patterns taking shape in children: Emma's determined rebuilding after her tower falls demonstrates her emerging understanding of boundaries and impact; Maya's careful observation before joining a group reveals her approach to safety and threat; Sofia's adjustments after receiving social feedback show her developing sense of belonging and worth. Through countless such interactions, these emotional responses crystallize into the stable personality structures we recognize as types.

The Superego's Role

As development progresses, these primary emotions become enlisted by the superego in its mission to keep us "acceptable" and "safe." What began as natural, protective responses become bound up in complex patterns of self-regulation:

- Anger gets channeled into self-criticism
- Fear becomes anticipatory anxiety
- Shame transforms into chronic self-doubt

Understanding this process gives us an unprecedented opportunity. By observing our children's emotional development and conflicts, we can witness personality patterning as it happens. More importantly, we can bring presence, awareness, and curiosity to these crucial moments, supporting:

- Flexibility in emotional response
- Resilience in facing challenges
- Plasticity in pattern formation

In the following chapters, we'll explore each primary emotion in depth, examining its vital role in development and how it becomes enlisted by the superego in maintaining personality patterns. We'll see how:

- Anger, which begins as pure life force and boundary-setting, becomes transformed into self-criticism and rigid standards
- Fear, originally a protective wisdom, evolves into anticipatory anxiety and complex control strategies
- Shame, initially a social guidance system, develops into an elaborate architecture of self-judgment and worth-management

By understanding this process—how these essential emotions become bound up in the superego's mission of keeping us "in the box"—we gain unprecedented opportunities to support healthy development. By observing our children's emotional experiences and conflicts, we can witness personality patterning as it happens and the formation of the inner critic that will shape their relationship with themselves. As we explore each emotion, we'll discover how to:

- Support its vital developmental role
- Recognize when it's becoming enlisted in rigid patterns
- Maintain flexibility in emotional response
- Help prevent its transformation into fixed self-criticism

Anger	**Fear**	**Shame**
Irritation	Anxiety	Embarrassment
Frustration	Panic	Humiliation
Resentment	Dread	Guilt
Rage	Apprehension	Regret
Fury	Terror	Disgrace
Annoyance	Nervousness	Remorse
Hostility	Worry	Mortification
Bitterness	Unease	Dishonor
Contempt	Phobia	Self-loathing
Outrage	Paranoia	Inferiority
Vexation	Alarm	Stigma
Wrath	Hesitation	Awkwardness
Indignation	Trepidation	Inadequacy
Exasperation	Agitation	Defeat

Reflection

Take a few quiet moments to explore how anger, fear, and shame move through your relationship with your child. Consider how your Type's pattern influences your relationship with these fundamental forces.

Your Emotional Inheritance

Notice your natural responses.

- Which of these emotions does your Type manage most actively?
- Where do you feel most comfortable or uncomfortable?
- How might your pattern with these emotions influence your child?
- What did you learn about these emotions in your childhood?

The Living Laboratory

Consider a recent emotional moment with your child.

- What happened in your body?
- How did your pattern want to respond?
- Where did you find flexibility?
- What helped you stay present?

Remember: These emotions serve vital developmental purposes. The goal isn't to prevent them but to support their healthy expression while maintaining enough flexibility for growth.

Take time to write about what support your pattern needs to hold space for these primary emotions in your parenting.

Your Notes

Chapter 4

Anger—Life Force in Action

Anger shows up when a child's boundaries are crossed—even if they don't have the words to say it.

As we explore anger, we'll discover how this fundamental life force energizes healthy development and transforms into the superego's system of self-regulation. We'll see how early experiences with acceptance influence our relationship with anger and how both shape the foundation of personality development.

At its core, anger is about life force (aggression), a distortion of our essential vital energy that helps us define ourselves and have an impact in the world. Watch three-year-old Marcus building with blocks. With each careful placement, his concentration deepens. The tower grows taller until—crash! A slight bump sends it tumbling. Marcus's face flushes, his tiny fists clench, and he screams with primal rage.

In this moment of anger's emergence, we see both the individual and the family ecosystem at work. Marcus's raw expression reveals his natural relationship with anger, influenced by his secure attachment with Lisa (8) and David (9). But watch how this individual expression immediately activates the family's anger ecology:

- Lisa immediately feels her energy rise to match Marcus's intensity. "It's okay to be mad!" she declares, her comfort with anger amplifying the emotional energy in the room. While creating space for anger in the family ecosystem, her response may overwhelm rather than contain the emotion.
- David feels his body tense, his pattern urging him to dampen the intensity. "Let's build it again together," he suggests quickly, hoping to dissolve the anger through peaceful activity. Within the family system, this response teaches that anger needs immediate soothing rather than acknowledgment.

The Body Triad (Types Eight, Nine, and One) reveals how humans naturally relate to anger and life force energy. Each type in this triad has a characteristic way of managing the body's relationship with force and impact. The patterns we see in Type Eight—

moving toward or away from anger—illuminate something essential about how all personality structures manage this vital energy.

This everyday moment illuminates how anger operates as an isolated emotion and a profound architect of personality. Watch closely, and you can see three distinct patterns forming: Marcus's pure expression of life force, Lisa's amplification through engagement, and David's dampening through peace-seeking. Each represents a different strategy for managing anger—strategies that, repeated over time, become core personality patterns.

The Nature of Anger

The Enneagram reveals that anger is fundamentally about life force (which is aggressive and expansive)—the vital energy of existence. Building on the foundations of acceptance and attachment we've explored, anger emerges as the energy that helps children define themselves and their boundaries. Consider the following expressions of healthy anger in different children.

Raw Life Force (6-18 months)

Watch how parents' patterns influence their children's early anger expression:

- Emma forcefully pushes away food she doesn't want, her natural assertion meeting Sarah's (1) discomfort with "messy" emotions. Sarah feels her pattern activate—the urge to quickly clean and restore order—but today, she chooses to breathe through her tension, allowing Emma's healthy self-expression.
- Maya cries out when her movement is restricted, her protest encountering Priya's (5) tendency toward withdrawal. While Priya's pattern urges distance from the intensity, she practices staying present, supporting Maya's natural boundary-setting.
- Sofia expresses clear preferences through sound and gesture, her emotional force meeting Ana's (2) helping pattern. Ana notices her impulse to soothe and fix, choosing instead to witness Sofia's authentic expression.

Boundary Formation (18-36 months)

Marcus's emphatic "No!" to unwanted sharing reveals his natural assertion and adaptation to his parents' patterns. Lisa (8) feels pride in his strength, while David (9) tenses at the potential conflict. Their contrasting responses create the ecosystem where Marcus learns to navigate his anger.

Watch how different parent-child pairs handle this crucial developmental stage:

- Emma's physical stance when claiming her space meets Sarah's (1) work with control patterns. Sarah practices allowing natural assertion while maintaining appropriate structure.
- Maya's protests during bedtime battles encounter Priya's (5) growing emotional engagement. Through conscious effort, Priya maintains connection while respecting Maya's need to express opposition.

Social Integration (3-6 years)

By this stage, children's anger expression reflects sophisticated adaptation to their family ecosystem:

- Lucas, learning to express disagreement, encounters Rachel's (3) complex relationship with conflict. Her pattern emphasizes looking good over authentic expression, but she creates space for Lucas's real feelings through her inner work.
- Marcus protecting a younger child shows how he has integrated Lisa's (8) protective strength with David's (9) peaceful presence. Their combined influence helps him develop nuanced ways of using his force.

Understanding Anger's Developmental Journey

Birth to 12 Months: The Raw Force Emerges

Four-month-old Maya arches her back and screams when her mother tries to put her down. This isn't just fussiness—it's her first experiment with protest, with saying "No" to what doesn't feel right. Her anger is pure life force, unmediated by thought or social conditioning.

Watch how different parent patterns shape the environment. Priya and Raj's response creates Maya's early anger ecosystem.

Priya's (5) tendency to step back and analyze leads her to:

- Question the intensity of Maya's response

- Create distance from the emotional force
- Seek understanding over engagement
- Miss opportunities for emotional holding

While Raj's (7) pattern adds another layer:

- Quick movement to distract from difficulty
- Reframing anger as excitement
- Avoiding the full force of feelings
- Missing chances for deep connection

Their combined influence on Maya's expression shows how children adapt to their parents' patterns from the earliest months. Maya learns that strong emotions lead to either analytical distance or quick deflection, shaping her emerging relationship with anger.

1-3 Years: The "No" Phase Reshapes the Family Field

Two-year-old Marcus stands firmly, face set with determination: "No bath!" This isn't defiance for its sake; it's the vital energy of separation-individuation at work. His whole body expresses the emerging force of his individual will, shaped by his secure attachment with Lisa (8) and David (9).

Watch how different parent patterns influence this stage.

Lisa's Type Eight approach:

- Respects the direct force
- Engages with the energy
- Sets clear boundaries
- Allows strong expression

While David's Type Nine tendencies:

- Seek peaceful resolution
- Offer gentle alternatives

- Avoid direct confrontation
- Look for compromise

Their combined response creates an ecosystem in which Marcus learns how directly he can express opposition, what intensity levels are acceptable when force meets resistance, and how conflict is resolved.

3-6 Years: The Social Field Expands

Five-year-old Emma comes home furious because another child wouldn't share the coveted red paint at art time. Her anger now involves complex social understanding, emerging values, and balancing her wants with others' needs. Watch how her parents' patterns influence her anger expression.

Sarah's (1) approach tends to:

- Focus on "appropriate" expression
- Teach proper responses
- Emphasize fairness
- Guide toward improvement

While Michael's (6) patterns:

- Worry about social impact
- Seek alliance-building
- Support careful assertion
- Look for safe solutions

Their combined influence helps Emma learn how to navigate anger in social settings, find appropriate channels for expressing her emotions, maintain relationships, and develop conflict-resolution skills.

The Power of "No"

The word "no" carries profound weight—not just for toddlers but also for adults. A parent's relationship with "no" often mirrors their history of hearing and expressing it. During the separation/individuation phase (18-24 months), this dynamic takes center stage as the child begins asserting autonomy. How parents respond to their toddler's emphatic "no" can either reinforce the child's sense of agency or create conflict.

While it's crucial for parents not to take "no" personally and to grow their tolerance for frustration, it's equally important to remain steadfast in maintaining boundaries. Clear, consistent limits provide children with a sense of security and help them understand the natural limits of the world. Striking this balance fosters both autonomy and a foundation of trust and safety.

As the ecosystem expands, the family system intersects with the school system, introducing new influences and dynamics.

Individual Development

Watch how different children navigate this stage:

Lucas learning to:

- Express frustration appropriately while managing Rachel's (3) focus on appearances
- Navigate peer conflicts within a success-oriented framework
- Assert needs clearly while maintaining social standing
- Balance authentic feelings with performance expectations

Sofia developing:

- Emotional expression skills shaped by Ana's (2) helping pattern
- Friendship navigation influenced by Carlos's (4) intensity
- Complex social strategies combining connection and uniqueness

- Need articulation balancing helping and being special

Maya mastering:

- Boundary setting within Priya's (5) analytical framework
- Quiet assertion reflecting her adaptation to withdrawal patterns
- Clear communication balanced with careful observation
- Space maintenance while managing connection

Each Family Ecosystem Adapts

Watch how Sarah and Michael create an environment where Emma's anger can be expressed within appropriate boundaries. Sarah works with her Type One focus on correctness by creating clear but flexible channels for emotional expression. At the same time, Michael balances his Type Six concern for security by supporting brave expression while maintaining safety.

The Patel Family (5 & 7):

- Balances observation with engagement
- Creates space for processing feelings
- Supports emotional exploration
- Maintains emotional containment

Observe how Priya and Raj develop an ecosystem where Maya can explore anger at her own pace. Priya works with her Type Five tendency toward withdrawal by staying present during emotional intensity, while Raj transforms his Type Seven impulse to deflect discomfort into creating safe spaces for emotional processing.

The Chen Family (8 & 9):

- Balances strength with peace
- Develops power with gentleness
- Supports direct expression
- Maintains relational harmony

Watch how Lisa and David create an environment where Marcus can express strong emotions while maintaining connection. Lisa works with her Type Eight intensity by moderating her force while honoring his natural strength. At the same time, David transforms his Type Nine peace-seeking into steady presence during conflict rather than withdrawal.

The Rodriguez Family (2 & 4):

- Integrates emotional depth with care
- Develops nuanced feeling recognition
- Supports authentic expression
- Maintains relational safety

Observe how Ana and Carlos develop an ecosystem where Sofia can explore her complex emotional landscape. Ana works with her Type Two tendency to soothe by creating space for full emotional expression without rushing to fix. At the same time, Carlos balances his Type Four intensity by containing emotions without amplifying their drama.

The Smith Family (3 & 1):

- Channels force into achievement
- Creates structured outlets
- Supports productive expression
- Maintains clear boundaries

Watch how Rachel and James create an environment where Lucas can transform anger into motivated action. Rachel works with her Type Three focus on performance by validating emotions beyond their productivity, while James balances his Type One correctness by accepting messy emotional expression while maintaining appropriate guidelines.

Understanding how your Type patterns create your family's emotional ecosystem gives you unprecedented opportunities to support your child's healthy relationship with anger. Each family develops its unique approach to this vital emotion, shaped by the parents' patterns but maintaining enough flexibility for the child's authentic expression to flourish.

The Body Triad Patterns

The Enneagram's Body Triad (Types Eight, Nine, and One) illuminates three fundamental ways humans relate to anger and life force energy. While we never type young children, understanding these patterns helps us recognize how individual anger styles interact with family systems to create distinctive emotional environments.

The Direct Force (Type Eight Pattern)

Watch Lisa's (8) interaction with Marcus's anger. Like a strong river flowing straight to the sea, this pattern represents anger in its most natural, unmediated form. When Marcus forcefully protests sharing his favorite truck, Lisa's instinctive response validates his right to set boundaries while helping him find appropriate expression.

Family Ecosystem Impact:

- Creates an environment of direct engagement
- Makes anger visible and present in the system
- Challenges others' comfort with confrontation
- Often forces family members to define their relationship with power

System Response:

- Family members may amplify or dampen their anger in response
- Different subsystems might form (e.g., "the loud ones" and "the quiet ones")
- Power dynamics become more explicit
- Conflict handling becomes a central family theme

Daily moments reveal this pattern as Marcus expresses frustration about bedtime, testing the boundaries of his emotions and limits. Lisa (8) responds with direct engagement, meeting his frustration head-on and shaping how the interaction unfolds. David (9) balances the dynamic with a peaceful presence, offering a contrast that helps regulate the emotional tone.

The Peaceful Merger (Type Nine Pattern)

Observe David's (9) response to anger in the family system. Like a stream disappearing underground, this pattern shows how anger can merge with the desire for harmony. When Marcus expresses frustration about sharing, David's natural inclination is to smooth things over, potentially teaching that anger should be avoided rather than expressed.

Family Ecosystem Impact:

- Creates an environment prioritizing peace and harmony
- Makes anger less visible in the system
- Develops patterns of conflict avoidance
- Often leads family members to submerge their own needs

System Response:

- Family members may suppress their anger to maintain peace
- Different family members might become "anger carriers" for the system
- Underlying tensions build without clear expression
- Conflict resolution becomes indirect or delayed

Daily life reveals this pattern as David responds to Marcus's protests by redirecting or accommodating rather than engaging directly with the frustration. This creates a complex dynamic where anger may go underground rather than finding healthy expression. Lisa (8) balances this with her direct approach, creating a system where Marcus experiences both engagement with and diffusion of emotional intensity.

The Righteous Improver (Type One Pattern)

Watch Sarah's (1) interaction with Emma's anger. Like a carefully engineered canal system, this pattern shows anger channeled into improvement. When Emma becomes frustrated with her artwork, Sarah's instinct is to turn the moment into a learning opportunity, potentially transforming raw anger into a drive for betterment.

Family Ecosystem Impact:

- Creates an environment focused on doing things "right"
- Develops complex systems for improvement
- Builds structured approaches to emotion
- Often leads to critiquing as a family pattern

System Response:

- Family members may internalize high standards
- Criticism becomes a primary mode of interaction
- Power operates through correctness
- Anger gets transmuted into improvement projects

Daily life reveals this pattern as Emma's frustration meets Sarah's (1) structured approach, creating a dynamic between emotional expression and order. Michael's (6) anxiety interacts with the family's standards, adding another layer of sensitivity and caution.

The Heart Center Patterns

The Enneagram's Heart Triad (Types Two, Three, and Four) illuminates three fundamental ways humans relate to shame and image. Understanding these patterns helps us recognize how different emotional styles interact with family systems to create distinctive emotional environments.

The Helping Pattern (Type Two)

Sofia's emotional outburst meets Ana's (2) pattern of managing anger through helping and connection. Without awareness, Ana might rush to soothe difficult feelings, transform anger into neediness, manage emotions through helping, and miss opportunities for healthy assertion. Watch their patterns interweave.

Family Ecosystem Impact:

- Creates an environment of emotional management
- Makes anger appear as neediness in the system

- Develops patterns of indirect expression
- Often leads family members to disguise needs as help

System Response:

- Family members may learn to get needs met through helping
- Different roles emerge around who helps and who receives
- Emotional authenticity becomes secondary to connection
- Conflict gets resolved through relationship repair

Daily life reveals this pattern as Sofia learns to express anger through relationship dynamics rather than direct assertion. When upset about sharing a toy, she might say "I wanted to help you play with it" rather than simply stating her desire to keep it. Ana responds by emphasizing connection, teaching that relationship maintenance takes precedence over raw emotional expression.

The Achievement Pattern (Type Three)

Watch Lucas during a moment of frustration with a puzzle. His anger meets Rachel's (3) emotional management pattern through performance and success. Without awareness, Rachel might quickly redirect to achievement, transform anger into competitive drive, manage emotions through doing, and miss opportunities for authentic feeling. Their shared relationship with anger reveals itself.

Family Ecosystem Impact:

- Creates an environment of productivity and success
- Makes anger appear as determination in the system
- Develops patterns of emotion-to-action conversion
- Often leads family members to channel feelings into results

System Response:

- Family members learn to transform emotions into accomplishments
- Different roles emerge around who performs and who validates
- Emotional expression becomes tied to productive outcomes
- Conflict gets resolved through goal-oriented solutions

Daily life reveals this pattern as Lucas learns to channel frustration into achievement rather than expressing it directly. When angry about a playdate ending, he might say "I'm going to build an even better fort next time" rather than simply expressing disappointment. Rachel responds by focusing on future success, teaching that emotions gain validity when directed toward achievements.

The Depth Pattern (Type Four)

Sofia's anger also encounters Carlos's (4) pattern of intensifying emotional experience. Without awareness, Carlos might amplify emotional drama, transform anger into emotional depth, create significant meaning from conflict, and miss opportunities for simple resolution. Watch how these patterns dance together:

Family Ecosystem Impact:

- Creates an environment of emotional significance
- Makes anger appear as meaningful intensity in the system
- Develops patterns of dramatic expression
- Often leads family members to intensify feelings

System Response:

- Family members learn that emotional depth signifies importance
- Different roles emerge around who expresses and who witnesses
- Emotional uniqueness becomes prized over common experience
- Conflict gets transformed into meaningful narrative

Daily life reveals this pattern as Sofia learns to give her anger special meaning rather than simply experiencing it. When upset about a friend's comment, she might create an elaborate story about feeling misunderstood rather than expressing straightforward hurt. Carlos responds by honoring the emotional depth, teaching that feelings gain validity through their intensity and uniqueness.

The Head Center Patterns

The Enneagram's Head Triad (Types Five, Six, and Seven) illuminates three fundamental ways humans relate to fear and anxiety. Understanding these patterns helps us recognize how different cognitive styles interact with family systems to create distinctive emotional environments.

The Observer Pattern (Type Five)

Watch Maya's anger encounter Priya's (5) pattern of managing emotions through withdrawal and analysis. Their dynamic reveals itself when Maya's frustration meets her mother's tendency to create distance. Without awareness, Priya might step back to analyze the anger, transform emotion into understanding, create distance from intensity, and miss opportunities for emotional engagement.

Family Ecosystem Impact:

- Creates an environment of intellectual processing
- Makes anger appear as a problem to solve in the system
- Develops patterns of emotional distancing
- Often leads family members to intellectualize feelings

System Response:

- Family members learn to process emotions through understanding
- Different roles emerge around who explains and who experiences
- Emotional containment becomes valued over expression
- Conflict gets resolved through analysis rather than engagement

Daily life reveals this pattern as Maya learns to observe and analyze her anger rather than fully expressing it. When frustrated about not being included in play, she might watch from a distance and develop theories about why it happened rather than directly engaging. Priya responds with explanations and perspective, teaching that understanding emotions is more important than expressing them.

The Security Pattern (Type Six)

Emma's anger also meets Michael's (6) complex relationship with force and authority. Without awareness, Michael might scan for danger in conflict, transform anger into anxiety, seek alliance in difficulty, and miss opportunities for direct assertion. Watch their patterns interact.

Family Ecosystem Impact:

- Creates an environment of cautious expression
- Makes anger appear as worry in the system
- Develops patterns of checking and confirming
- Often leads family members to seek support for feelings

System Response:

- Family members learn to process anger through alliances
- Different roles emerge around who questions and who reassures
- Emotional validation becomes critical to expression
- Conflict gets resolved through collective processing

Daily life reveals this pattern as Emma learns to check her anger against others' reactions rather than trusting her direct experience. When upset about a boundary, she might ask "Is it okay to be mad about this?" rather than simply feeling her frustration. Michael responds with careful validation, teaching that emotions need verification and support to be safely expressed.

The Option Pattern (Type Seven)

Watch how Raj's (7) pattern influences Maya's relationship with anger. Their dynamic emerges when Maya's frustration meets her father's tendency to maintain options and reframe experiences. Without awareness, Raj might quickly move to positive reframing, transform anger into excitement, create multiple escape routes, and miss opportunities for emotional depth.

Family Ecosystem Impact:

- Creates an environment of positive possibilities
- Makes anger appear as energy in the system
- Develops patterns of quick emotional transitions
- Often leads family members to reframe difficult feelings

System Response:

- Family members learn to transform negative emotions into positive ones
- Different roles emerge around who uplifts and who experiences
- Emotional agility becomes valued over sustained processing
- Conflict gets resolved through redirection and reframing

Daily life reveals this pattern as Maya learns to quickly transform anger into new possibilities rather than staying with difficult feelings. When frustrated about a broken toy, she might immediately say "Let's make something better!" rather than expressing disappointment. Raj responds with enthusiastic alternatives, teaching that emotional pain can be escaped through positive reframing.

Working with Anger Patterns

Rather than fixing or controlling anger, our role as parents is to support its healthy expression while creating an ecosystem where all family members can grow. This requires attention to both individual patterns and system dynamics. Watch how different families create supportive containers.

The Chen Family Dynamic (Types 8 and 9)

When Marcus expresses intense anger about his fallen tower, Lisa (8) and David (9) create a balanced response through contrasting patterns. Lisa's natural comfort with strong emotions allows her to stay present with intensity, while David's peaceful presence helps maintain calm containment. Together, they create designated spaces where Marcus can:

- Express strong emotions safely

- Learn to regulate intensity
- Develop healthy boundaries
- Find his way back to calm

The Connor Family Approach (Types 1 and 6)

Sarah (1) and Michael (6) support Emma's anger expression through conscious attention to their patterns. Sarah works with her perfectionist tendency by creating structured spaces that allow for emotional messiness. Michael's anxiety about conflict leads him to develop clear but flexible guidelines. Their combined influence helps Emma learn that anger can be contained and authentic.

- Express emotions within clear guidelines
- Learn to balance control and release
- Develop organized ways to process feelings
- Find her way through frustration

The Patel Family System (Types 5 and 7)

Maya's expression of anger meets her parents' different approaches to emotional intensity. Priya (5) recognizes her pattern of withdrawal when Maya's feelings run high, consciously working to maintain connection while respecting Maya's need for space. Raj (7) notices his tendency to quickly redirect or reframe Maya's anger, learning to stay present with difficult emotions instead.

Together, they create an environment where Maya learns to:

- Process feelings without complete withdrawal
- Express anger while maintaining reflection
- Navigate between thought and action
- Find her balance between distance and engagement

The Rodriguez Family Balance (Types 2 and 4)

Sofia encounters her parents' contrasting approaches to emotional expression. Ana (2) works with her helping pattern that wants to immediately soothe anger away, while

Carlos (4) manages his tendency to amplify emotional intensity. Their combined awareness creates space for Sofia to discover her authentic relationship with anger rather than adapting to either extreme.

Through conscious parenting, they learn to:

- Allow natural emotional expression
- Support rather than manage feelings
- Maintain connection through conflict
- Create space for authentic experience

Working with Different Anger Expressions

When Marcus expresses anger through intense physical movement, Lisa (8) and David (9) must each work with their patterns. Lisa felt her instinct to match his intensity, while David noticed his urge to dampen the force. Their conscious awareness creates space for Marcus to develop his relationship with anger's energy.

Lisa learns to:

- Support strong expression while teaching boundaries
- Maintain protective presence without overwhelming
- Allow intensity while ensuring safety
- Model healthy use of force

David balances this by:

- Offering steady presence without withdrawal
- Supporting peaceful resolution without suppression
- Maintaining connection through conflict
- Creating calm containment

When Emma encounters frustration with her artwork, Sarah (1) and Michael (6) face their patterns around anger. Sarah works with her perfectionistic response to emotional "messiness," while Michael manages his anxiety about conflict. Their combined effort helps Emma learn that anger can be contained and authentic

Sarah practices:

- Allowing natural expression despite her discomfort
- Supporting process over perfection
- Maintaining structure without rigidity
- Creating space for real feelings

When Maya shows frustration through quiet withdrawal, Priya (5) and Raj (7) encounter distinct patterns around emotional expression. Priya recognizes her tendency to analyze rather than engage, while Raj notices his impulse to shift the mood quickly. Their awareness allows Maya to find her authentic way of expressing anger.

Priya works with her pattern by:

- Maintaining emotional presence despite her urge to retreat
- Engaging directly rather than just observing
- Staying connected while respecting boundaries
- Supporting rather than analyzing feelings

Raj balances this by:

- Allowing difficult emotions to exist
- Staying present instead of seeking escape
- Supporting authentic expression
- Creating space for natural processing

When Sofia expresses anger through emotional intensity, Ana (2) and Carlos (4) must each manage their patterns. Ana feels her helping instinct activate—wanting to immediately soothe and fix—while Carlos notices his tendency to amplify the emotional drama. Their conscious work creates space for Sofia to develop her relationship with anger.

Through their combined awareness, they learn to:

- Allow feelings without rushing to resolve them
- Support expression without escalation
- Maintain connection without managing
- Create space for authentic emotional experience

Integration and Moving Forward

Remember that working with anger isn't about control but integration. Each family finds their way of supporting healthy anger expression while maintaining flexibility in patterns.

The Connor Family Balance (Types 1 and 6)

Sarah (1) and Michael (6) work with their patterns to support Emma's relationship with anger.

Through conscious attention, Sarah learns to create clear boundaries that allow for emotional messiness. She works with her perfectionist pattern that wants to "correct" Emma's anger instead of creating space where feelings can be contained and authentic. Michael's anxiety about conflict leads him to develop guidelines that offer security while remaining flexible. Their combined influence helps Emma learn that:

- Strong feelings can exist within structure
- Expression doesn't require perfection
- Anger can be both safe and real
- Emotions need space to unfold

The Patel Family Integration (Types 5 and 7)

Priya (5) and Raj (7) support Maya's development by integrating their different approaches to emotional intensity.

Priya works to maintain connection despite her withdrawal pattern, while Raj learns to stay present when facing difficulty rather than seeking quick solutions. Their conscious effort creates an environment where Maya can discover her unique expression of anger. Through their combined awareness, Maya learns that:

- Feelings can be processed without complete withdrawal
- Expression doesn't require immediate resolution
- Anger deserves time and space
- Emotions can be both thought about and felt

The Chen Family Integration (Types 8 and 9)

Lisa (8) and David (9) balance their contrasting patterns to support Marcus's relationship with anger.

Lisa works with her comfort with intensity, learning to maintain a protective presence without overwhelming. David practices staying engaged despite his peace-seeking pattern. Their conscious integration helps Marcus discover how strength and gentleness can coexist. Through their balanced approach, Marcus learns that:

- Force can be both strong and contained
- Expression can honor both power and peace
- Anger can protect without dominating
- Emotions can be intense yet regulated

The Rodriguez Family Dynamic (Types 2 and 4)

Ana (2) and Carlos (4) combine their patterns to support Sofia's emotional development.

Ana practices allowing feelings to exist without rushing to fix them, while Carlos works with his tendency to amplify emotional drama. Their conscious effort creates space for Sofia to find her authentic relationship with anger rather than adapting to either extreme. Through their integrated approach, Sofia discovers that:

- Feelings don't always need fixing
- Expression can be deep without drama
- Anger can exist without resolution

- Emotions are valid without amplification

The Smith Family Approach (Types 3 and 1)

Rachel (3) and James (1) work with their patterns to support Lucas's emotional expression.

Rachel learns to value emotions beyond their productive outcomes, while James practices accepting messiness in emotional expression rather than seeking immediate order. Their conscious effort creates an environment where Lucas can experience anger as natural rather than something to be channeled or corrected. Through their combined approach, Lucas discovers that:

- Feelings have value beyond their results
- Expression doesn't require achievement
- Anger can exist without being productive
- Emotions need not be perfectly structured

Each family's journey with anger is unique, shaped by the parents' patterns and the child's natural expression. The goal isn't to eliminate anger but to support its healthy integration while maintaining flexibility in response.

Supporting Healthy Development

The Foundation Years (0-3)

Sarah (1) and Michael (6) help young Emma by:

- Accepting natural anger expression
- Supporting clear communication
- Allowing messy emotions
- Maintaining loving presence

Lisa (8) and David (9) support toddler Marcus through:

- Accepting strong feelings
- Supporting healthy boundaries
- Allowing protective impulses
- Maintaining balanced connection

The Patterning Years (3-6)

Priya (5) and Raj (7) work with Maya by:

- Accepting quiet strength
- Supporting clear expression
- Allowing natural rhythm
- Maintaining steady presence

Ana (2) and Carlos (4) help Sofia through:

- Accepting emotional range
- Supporting authentic needs
- Allowing independent expression
- Maintaining loving connection

Building Long-Term Resilience

The goal isn't to eliminate anger but to support its integration while maintaining flexibility in response. By understanding how anger patterns form and how they can remain flexible, we help our children develop:

- Trust in their protective instincts
- Confidence in their boundaries
- Flexibility in their responses
- Resilience in their relationships

Moving from our exploration of anger to examining fear, notice how your Type's approach to force and boundary-setting influences your relationship with protection and safety. Your particular way of handling anger—whether through expression, suppression, or redirection—shapes how you create an environment of security for your child. In the next chapter, we'll discover how your Type's characteristic approach to fear creates the personal ecology in which your child develops their relationship with uncertainty and threat. We'll see how your patterns around safety influence your child's emerging strategies for navigating an unpredictable world.

Reflection

Take a few quiet moments to explore your relationship with anger—your own and your child's. This powerful emotion shapes how boundaries form and how authentic expression develops.

Your Pattern's Influence

Consider your automatic responses to anger.

- What happens in your body when anger arises?
- How does your type typically manage this energy?
- Where do you feel challenged by your child's anger?
- What helps you stay present with this force?

The Dance of Boundaries

Notice how you respond to your child's assertions.

- What arises when they say "No!"?
- How does your pattern handle their resistance?
- Where do you find flexibility?
- What supports your ability to hold space?

Take time to write about a recent interaction involving anger. What did you notice about:

- Your automatic responses?
- Your child's experience?

Remember: Anger serves vital developmental purposes. Your child needs to experience your healthy relationship with this force to develop their own.

Take time to write about what support for which your pattern needs to hold space for these primary emotions in your parenting.

Your Notes

Chapter 5

Fear—The Foundation of Protection

A child's greatest fear isn't the dark—it's being alone in it.

As we explore fear, we'll discover how this vital life force interacts with our protective instincts. We'll see how early experiences with anger influence our relationship with fear and how both emotions work together in healthy development.

The fear of annihilation lies at the heart of all ego structures—this fundamental anxiety drives ego formation and maintenance. The Head Triad (Types Five, Six, and Seven) reveals essential ways humans respond to this core fear. Each type in this triad has a characteristic way of managing the mind's relationship with uncertainty and threat.

Type Six, at the core of the Head triad, reveals something universal about how all personality structures manage anxiety. The mind naturally gravitates toward binary responses: fight or flight, approach or avoid, engage or withdraw. This binary processing differs from how the Heart Center manages shame or how the Body Center handles anger. While the heart doesn't think in binaries (Type Three's neutral position isn't split) and the body tends toward merging (Type Nine), the mind naturally divides experience into opposing choices.

Picture this: Four-year-old Maya stands frozen at the top of the playground slide, her hands gripping the rails, tears threatening to spill. Below, her mother Priya (5), feels her anxiety rising, urging her to analyze and explain rather than be present. This moment—so ordinary in early childhood—illuminates how each child develops a unique ecology of fear, a complex personal system of how they perceive, assess, and respond to threats in their environment.

Fear isn't just one emotion among many. Building on the foundations of acceptance, attachment, and healthy anger (aggression) we've explored, fear emerges as the basic emotion underlying all ego development, the foundation upon which personality structures are built. Every personality pattern, every coping strategy, and every adaptive behavior stems from each child's unique ecology of fear and how that ecology develops through interaction with their environment.

When children desperately seek attention, they're not manipulative; they're responding to a genuine threat within their fear landscape. When they become rigid about routines or possessions, they're attempting to create safe territories in an overwhelming world. When they rage against limitations or collapse in apparent overreaction to minor disappointments, they're experiencing the full intensity of a developing psyche for whom every experience carries existential weight.

This fundamental reality—that each child develops a complex ecology of fear—reveals itself in the nine patterns the Enneagram describes. Each pattern represents a different way of constructing and maintaining a personal ecology of fear. What matters isn't eliminating these patterns but supporting enough flexibility so they don't become rigid, limiting responses.

Understanding this transforms how we view early childhood behavior. The clingy child, the defiant child, the perfectionist child, the people-pleasing child—all are showing us different strategies for managing their ecology of fear. Our role isn't to eliminate these strategies but to understand them through the Enneagram's wisdom while supporting their healthy expression.

This deeper understanding helps us move beyond simple behavior management to supporting genuine developmental integration. When we recognize how each child constructs their unique ecology of fear, we can work with it more consciously, helping our child maintain access to fear's protective wisdom while developing the flexibility to engage fully with life.

Consider these different expressions of fear's protective wisdom.

Basic Safety (6-18 months)

Watch how parents support their children's natural protective responses:

- Emma startles at loud sounds, met by Sarah's (1) steady, containing presence
- Marcus shows distress with sudden movements, held by Lisa's (8) protective strength
- Sofia's whole body tenses at unfamiliar faces, soothed by Ana's (2)

emotional attunement

• Lucas's protest at being put down finds regulation through Rachel's (3) consistent response

Anticipatory Fear (18-36 months)

Notice how parental patterns influence developing safety awareness.

• Maya's mother Priya (5) validates her caution with unfamiliar dogs

• Emma's structured approach to new situations reflects Sarah's (1) support

• Marcus checks for his parents' presence, anchored by Lisa's (8) reliable strength

• Sofia's separation anxiety meets Ana's (2) emotional holding

Complex Fear Patterns (3-6 years)

Observe how parental patterns shape more sophisticated fear responses.

• Lucas's specific fears encounter Rachel's (3) growing acceptance of vulnerability

• Maya's worry scenarios meet Priya's (5) analytical containment

• Emma's performance anxiety interacts with Sarah's (1) work on perfectionism

• Sofia's social fears find understanding through Ana's (2) emotional attunement

Fear's Dual Nature

A child's ecology of fear develops through the interplay of two distinct yet interrelated aspects: objective fear, our built-in survival mechanism, and subjective fear, the mind's interpretive and pattern-making system. Understanding this dual nature helps us recognize how each child's ecology of fear takes shape and evolves.

When two-year-old Maya pulls back from a steep drop or five-year-old Marcus hesitates before approaching a growling dog, they're experiencing objective fear—our natural protective wisdom at work. This immediate, instinctive response to genuine threats forms the basic structure of their developing ecology of fear.

Watch how different parent patterns influence this natural protective system.

The Patel Family (Types 5 and 7)

Working with her Type Five tendency to analyze, Priya learns to stay emotionally present while supporting Maya's cautious assessment. Raj balances with his Type Seven capacity to make challenges feel manageable without dismissing legitimate concerns. Their combined presence helps Maya develop trust in her protective instincts and her ability to face challenges.

The Connor Family (Types 1 and 6)

Managing her Type One drive for correctness, Sarah learns to validate Emma's natural caution rather than imposing her standards of appropriate fear. Michael works with his Type Six vigilance to contain his anxiety without amplifying Emma's concerns. Their conscious effort helps Emma trust her natural protective instinct while learning safe ways to navigate social situations.

The Chen Family (Types 8 and 9)

Balancing her Type Eight protective force, Lisa learns to support Marcus's natural caution without pushing for toughness. David works with his Type Nine peace-seeking to stay engaged with discomfort rather than minimizing concerns. Their combined approach helps Marcus honor his protective instincts while maintaining connection during uncertainty.

The Rodriguez Family (Types 2 and 4)

Working with her Type Two helping pattern, Ana learns to witness Sofia's natural protective responses without rushing to fix or soothe. Carlos balances his Type Four intensity by containing his emotional reactions rather than amplifying Sofia's concerns. Their conscious presence helps Sofia trust her instinctive fear responses while maintaining emotional resilience.

The Smith Family (Types 1 and 3)

> Managing her Type Three achievement focus, Rachel learns to validate Lucas's natural caution without redirecting toward performance. James works with his Type One correctness to accept fear as appropriate rather than something to be improved. Their combined effort helps Lucas trust his protective instincts without needing to show competence in managing them.

Parents often mistake this natural protective system for timidity or excessive caution. When three-year-old Emma steps back from an aggressive child at the playground, she doesn't need Sarah (1) to convince her the child is friendly; she needs support in trusting her natural protective instinct while learning safe ways to interact with others.

The Architecture of Subjective Fear

Subjective fear emerges as children develop the capacity to imagine, remember, and create meaning from their experiences. This fear appears when four-year-old Marcus refuses to sleep in his room because of imagined monsters or when six-year-old Emma develops elaborate rituals to prevent bad things from happening.

Watch how different parenting patterns influence this development. Lisa (8) supports Marcus's nighttime fears by balancing protection with emotional validation, while David (9) brings a calm, steady presence that helps ease tension. Together, they create an environment where Marcus can:

- Develop confidence in facing fear
- Learn balanced safety assessment
- Build healthy coping strategies
- Grow emotional regulation skills

Subjective fear is particularly challenging because it operates through the same physiological systems as objective fear. To the child's body and nervous system, imagined threats feel as real as physical dangers. When five-year-old Sofia panics about being left at preschool, her racing heart, shallow breathing, and fight-flight response are physically identical to what she'd experience when facing a real threat.

The parent's work lies in learning to honor the reality of their child's physical experience of fear while supporting their developing discernment about what constitutes real versus imagined threat. They must maintain connection through fearful moments rather than dismissing or amplifying the fear while teaching healthy strategies for managing anxiety. This delicate balance requires parents to work consciously with their patterns around fear to provide both the safety and freedom their child needs to develop resilience.

Let's move into how these patterns develop into personal fear ecologies.

Head Center Influences

Priya's Type Five Pattern

Maya's environment is shaped by her mother's focus on managing being overwhelmed and intruded upon. Watch how Maya adapts to her mother's strategy:

- Learning to create knowledge territories
- Establishing observation posts
- Developing resource protection
- Maintaining safe distance

Her careful study before engagement, protected spaces for retreat, and structured approach to challenges reflect her adaptation to an environment where safety comes through understanding and preparation.

Raj's Type Seven Pattern

Maya's environment is also shaped by her father Raj's (7) approach to managing fear through reframing and options.

Watch how she adapts to this pattern:

- Learning to create escape routes
- Developing multiple options for handling situations
- Adopting positive reframe strategies
- Maintaining paths of movement

Between her parents' patterns—Priya's (5) analytical withdrawal and Raj's (7) quick movement to possibilities—Maya learns to navigate fear through careful assessment and ready alternatives. This isn't about Maya becoming a Five or Seven, but about developing strategies to adapt and secure connection within her family environment.

Michael's Type Six Pattern

Michael's (6) pattern influences Emma's relationship with uncertainty. Her routines mirror his strategies.

- Building alliance systems
- Creating checking protocols
- Establishing backup plans
- Maintaining vigilance

Watch how different parent patterns influence this development.

Lisa (8) supports Marcus's nighttime fears by balancing protection with emotional validation, while David (9) brings a calm, steady presence that helps ease tension. Together, they create an environment where Marcus can:

- Develop confidence in facing fears
- Learn balanced safety assessment
- Build healthy coping strategies
- Grow emotional regulation skills

Sarah (1) supports Emma's concern for correctness by balancing structure with flexibility, while Michael (6) brings careful preparation that helps manage uncertainty. Together, they create an environment where Emma can:

- Develop confidence in facing fears
- Learn balanced safety assessment
- Build healthy coping strategies
- Grow emotional regulation skills

Raj (7) supports Maya's exploration by balancing possibilities with present engagement, while Priya (5) brings thoughtful analysis that helps provide grounding. Together, they create an environment where Maya can:

- Develop confidence through possibilities
- Learn balanced option assessment
- Build healthy reframing skills
- Grow planning with presence integration

Subjective fear is particularly challenging because it operates through the same physiological systems as objective fear. To the child's body and nervous system, imagined threats feel as real as physical dangers. When five-year-old Sofia panics about being left at preschool, her racing heart, shallow breathing, and fight-flight response are physically identical to what she'd experience when facing a real threat.

The challenge for parents becomes learning to honor the reality of their child's physical experience of fear while supporting their developing discernment about what constitutes actual versus imagined threat. They must maintain connection through fearful moments rather than dismissing or amplifying the fear while teaching healthy strategies for managing anxiety. This delicate balance requires parents to work consciously with their patterns around fear to provide both the safety and freedom their child needs to develop resilience.

Heart Center Influences

Ana's Type Two Pattern

Ana's (2) pattern creates an environment where safety is secured through relationship and helping. Notice how Sofia adapts to this atmosphere:

- Learning to read and respond to others' needs
- Developing sophisticated emotional radar
- Creating connection through service
- Maintaining helpful presence

These aren't inherent traits but intelligent adaptations to an environment where connection comes through attunement to others' needs.

Rachel's Type Three Pattern

Watch how Lucas adapts to an environment where security comes through achievement and image management. His mother Rachel's (3) pattern creates an atmosphere where success and performance become linked to safety.

- Developing keen awareness of others' expectations
- Learning to adapt quickly to feedback
- Creating sophisticated success strategies
- Building performance-based security

These aren't Lucas's inherent traits but his intelligent adaptation to an environment where recognition and accomplishment are primary paths to connection.

Carlos's Type Four Pattern

Sofia's environment is further shaped by her father Carlos's (4) approach to managing fear through uniqueness and emotional depth. Notice how she adapts to this additional influence.

- Learning to transform ordinary moments into significant experiences
- Developing complex emotional narratives
- Creating special aspects of self
- Building identity through differentiation

Between her parents' patterns—Ana's (2) focus on helping and Carlos's (4) emphasis on uniqueness—Sofia learns to navigate her world through emotional attunement and personal distinction. This isn't about Sofia becoming a Type Two or Four but about developing strategies to secure connection within her family environment.

Body Center Influences

Lisa's Type Eight Pattern

Marcus's environment is significantly shaped by his mother Lisa's (8) approach to managing fear through power and protection. Notice how he adapts to this influence.

- Learning to establish clear territories

- Developing direct approaches to challenges
- Creating protective boundaries
- Building strength-based security

David's Type Nine Pattern

Marcus's environment is further shaped by his father David's (9) approach to managing fear through peace and harmony. Notice how he adapts to this additional influence.

- Learning to smooth over conflicts
- Developing merger strategies
- Creating comfortable spaces
- Building harmony-based security

Between his parents' patterns—Lisa's (8) emphasis on strength and David's (9) focus on peace—Marcus learns to navigate his world through assertion and accommodation. This isn't about Marcus becoming a Type Eight or Nine but about developing strategies to maintain connection within his family environment.

Sarah's Type One Pattern

Emma's environment is shaped by her mother Sarah's (1) approach to managing fear through correctness and improvement. Watch how she adapts to this atmosphere.

- Learning to create ordered spaces
- Developing careful checking systems
- Creating clear standards
- Building structure-based security

The Evolution of Personal Fear Ecology

These adaptive patterns don't appear all at once but evolve through distinct developmental stages. Watch how children refine their strategies for managing fear in response to their parents' patterns.

Early Formation (0-18 months)

During these foundational months, children begin adapting to their parents' ways of managing fear and creating safety.

Maya mirrors both parents' approaches:

- Her startle responses meet Priya's (5) careful analysis
- Her early protective behaviors encounter Raj's (7) quick reframes
- She begins developing strategies that combine observation with options
- Her safety mapping reflects both careful assessment and flexibility

Marcus adapts to his parents' contrasting styles:

- His physical responses meet Lisa's (8) emphasis on strength
- His early boundary testing encounters David's (9) peace-making
- He learns to navigate between assertion and accommodation
- His protective strategies blend force with harmony

Emma's early patterns show adaptation to parental influence:

- Her careful assessment mirrors Sarah's (1) attention to correctness
- Her reactions reflect structured approaches to safety
- She develops early strategies for managing uncertainty through order
- Her protective behaviors show emerging attention to standards

Pattern Reinforcement (18-36 months)

During these crucial years, children's adaptive strategies become more refined in response to their parents' patterns:

Sofia's adaptations to her parents deepen.

- Her connection-based safety strategies mirror Ana's (2) helping pattern

- Her emotional territory expands through Carlos's (4) emphasis on depth
- She develops increasingly sophisticated ways of securing connection
- Her safety map combines helpfulness with uniqueness

Lucas refines his responses to his environment.

- His performance-based strategies reflect Rachel's (3) achievement focus
- His security becomes increasingly linked to successful adaptation
- He develops more complex ways of reading and meeting expectations
- His safety becomes tied to recognition and accomplishment

Maya's adaptations become more sophisticated.

- Her observation-based strategies mirror Priya's (5) analytical approach
- Her quick reframes reflect Raj's (7) movement to possibilities
- She develops ways to combine careful assessment with options
- Her safety system balances withdrawal with engagement

Strategy Refinement (3-6 years)

During this period, children's adaptive patterns become more sophisticated and complex.

Emma's Evolution

Her adaptations to Sarah's (1) pattern become more elaborate.

- Her rules-based safety systems grow more complex
- Her checking routines become more detailed and systematic
- Her standards for safety become more nuanced
- Her strategies for creating order become more sophisticated

This emerges through Emma's elaborate checking routines before activities, increasingly detailed systems for ensuring correctness, complex standards for managing situations, and structured approaches to new experiences. Each behavior reflects her adaptation to an environment shaped by her mother's Type One pattern of creating safety through order and improvement.

Working with Fear Patterns

Understanding how children adapt to their parents' patterns transforms how we support their development. Rather than trying to eliminate fear or fix patterns, we aim to help children maintain access to fear's protective wisdom while developing flexible responses. Children adapting to different parental patterns need other types of support.

Different parental patterns require different approaches to supporting children's adaptive strategies.

The Cautious Observer (Maya)

Watch how Priya (5) and Raj (7) learn to support Maya's adaptations to their patterns.

Physical Space: Priya and Raj learn to create an environment that supports Maya's adaptations by establishing clear observation points that allow both distance and engagement, maintaining quiet areas for processing, developing gradual engagement zones, and establishing safe retreat spaces where she can regulate her energy and exposure.

Emotional Support: They learn to balance their contrasting patterns by respecting Maya's need for assessment while encouraging exploration, providing time for processing while maintaining connection, offering information without overwhelming, and balancing careful observation with gentle encouragement. This combined approach helps Maya develop flexible strategies for managing fear and engagement.

Maya's Development

Her adaptations to both parents' patterns show increasing sophistication.

- Her observation-based strategies (reflecting Priya's Type Five) become more detailed
- Her option-creating abilities (mirroring Raj's Type Seven) grow more complex
- Her information gathering becomes more systematic
- Her methods for managing overwhelm show greater flexibility

This appears through Maya's detailed information gathering before engagement, her complex systems for observing situations, elaborate strategies for maintaining comfortable distance, and sophisticated ways of keeping options open. Each behavior reflects her adaptation to Priya's (5) emphasis on understanding and Raj's (7) focus on maintaining options.

The Direct Engager (Marcus)

See how Lisa (8) and David (9) learn to balance their contrasting influences.

Physical Space: Lisa and David learn to create an environment that supports Marcus's adaptations by establishing clear areas for testing boundaries, creating protected zones for exploration, maintaining strong but flexible boundaries, and developing spaces that support both assertion and peace. This balanced approach reflects their work in integrating their contrasting patterns.

Emotional Support: They learn to support Marcus by validating his strength and sensitivity, helping him develop balanced assessments of situations, recognizing limits while encouraging growth, and celebrating wisdom in both action and restraint. Their combined approach helps Marcus develop flexible strategies that incorporate protection and harmony.

Maya's situation is unique because both parents operate from the Head Triad, where fear is the dominant emotion. While this double influence from the same triad might intensify her focus on mental strategies for managing fear, her parents' contrasting approaches—Priya's withdrawal and analysis versus Raj's movement and reframing —provide her with a broader repertoire of cognitive tools. This isn't about Maya becoming a Type Five or Seven, but about her developing sophisticated mental strategies for managing fear and anxiety.

Marcus's Development

His responses to his parents' contrasting patterns become more refined.

- His strength-based strategies (adapting to Lisa's Type Eight) become more nuanced
- His peace-making abilities (reflecting David's Type Nine) grow more sophisticated
- His boundary-setting becomes more flexible

- His protective responses show increasing complexity

This manifests through Marcus's increasingly sophisticated ways of asserting boundaries, his complex strategies for managing conflict, his more nuanced expression of strength, and his layered approaches to maintaining safety. Each behavior reflects his adaptation to the dynamic between Lisa's (8) emphasis on protection and David's (9) focus on peace.

Marcus's situation is similar to Maya's because both parents operate from the Body Triad, where anger is the dominant emotion. While this double influence from the same triad might intensify his focus on physical and instinctual strategies for managing fear, his parents' contrasting approaches—Lisa's assertion and protection versus David's merging and peace-making—provide him with a broader repertoire of body-based responses. This isn't about Marcus becoming a Type Eight or Nine, but about his developing sophisticated strategies for managing the energy of anger and the need for both strength and peace.

The Careful Planner (Emma)

Notice how Sarah (1) and Michael (6) learn to work with their patterns' influence.

Physical Space: Sarah and Michael learn to create an environment that supports Emma's adaptations by creating organized areas that still allow for exploration, maintaining clear but flexible procedure zones, developing structured spaces that permit spontaneity, and establishing safe areas for practice and experimentation. This balanced approach helps integrate their Type One and Type Six patterns.

Emotional Support: They learn to support Emma by validating caution while supporting natural development, providing structure without rigidity, recognizing readiness while allowing natural timing, and celebrating progress without demanding perfection. Their combined approach helps Emma develop flexible strategies that balance order with exploration.

Working with Common Challenges

The Overwhelmed Child

When six-year-old Sofia becomes paralyzed by social anxiety, Ana (2) and Carlos (4) learn to:

Provide Immediate Support: Ana and Carlos learn to help Sofia in anxious moments by offering calm presence without overwhelming her with help, containing emotions without dramatic escalation, presenting clear, simple choices without taking over, and supporting engagement while respecting her pace. This approach helps them balance their Type Two and Type Four tendencies to either rush in with help or amplify emotional intensity.

Develop Long-term Strategies: They support Sofia's growing confidence by creating gradual exposure opportunities, building skills through manageable steps, supporting success experiences, and fostering growing confidence. This balanced approach helps Sofia develop her flexible strategies for managing social anxiety while maintaining authentic connection.

In Sofia's situation, both parents operate from the Heart Triad, where shame is the dominant emotion. While this double influence from the same triad might intensify her focus on emotional and image-based strategies for managing fear, her parents' contrasting approaches—Ana's helping and connection versus Carlos's depth and uniqueness—provide her with a broader repertoire of emotional responses. This isn't about Sofia becoming a Type Two or Four, but about developing sophisticated strategies for managing emotional intensity and the need for connection and authenticity.

The Reckless Child

When five-year-old Marcus seems to ignore danger signals, Lisa (8) and David (9) learn to:

Provide Immediate Support: Lisa and David learn to help Marcus in risky moments by setting clear boundaries without overwhelming force, offering physical protection without controlling, using direct communication while maintaining connection, and allowing natural consequences within safe limits. This approach helps them balance their Type Eight and Type Nine tendencies to either control through force or avoid confrontation.

Develop Long-term Strategies: They support Marcus's growing judgment by teaching risk assessment without inducing anxiety, building danger recognition skills, developing protection awareness, and supporting balanced judgment. This combined approach helps Marcus develop flexible risk management strategies while maintaining confidence and awareness.

Supporting Different Fear Styles

Children with Head Center Parents

Parent Approach: For children adapting to Head Center patterns, parents learn to support development by providing information without overwhelming, allowing observation while maintaining connection, supporting analysis while encouraging engagement, and maintaining emotional presence alongside cognitive understanding. This balanced approach helps prevent withdrawal into pure mental processing.

Growth Support: These parents foster healthy development by building balanced assessment skills, helping children develop understanding without retreating from experience, creating knowledge that supports rather than replaces connection, and encouraging thoughtful engagement with experience. This integration allows children to build flexible strategies combining mental clarity and emotional presence.

This work requires particular attention from Head Center parents, who may naturally emphasize cognitive understanding over emotional engagement. The goal is to help children develop both capacities in balance.

Children with Heart Center Parents

Parent Approach: For children adapting to Heart Center patterns, parents learn to support development by offering emotional attunement without merging, providing relationship security while supporting independence, supporting connection without creating dependency, and maintaining emotional presence while allowing separation. This balanced approach helps prevent over-identification with emotions and relationships.

Growth Support: These parents foster healthy development by building emotional vocabulary without over-identifying, helping children develop relationship trust while maintaining boundaries, creating secure connection that allows for autonomy, and supporting balanced emotional navigation. This integration helps children develop flexible strategies, combining emotional intelligence and healthy independence.

This work requires particular attention from Heart Center parents, who may naturally emphasize emotional connection over healthy separation. The goal is to help children develop both capacities in balance.

Children with Body Center Parents

Parent Approach: For children adapting to Body Center patterns, parents learn to support development by creating clear boundaries without rigidity, providing physical security while allowing exploration, supporting direct engagement without overwhelming, and maintaining a strong presence while permitting vulnerability. This balanced approach helps prevent over-reliance on control or force.

Growth Support: These parents foster healthy development by building physical confidence balanced with sensitivity, helping children develop protection skills that include flexibility, creating action plans that allow for adjustment, and supporting direct handling of challenges while maintaining connection. This integration allows children to develop flexible strategies that combine strength with adaptability.

This work requires particular attention from Body Center parents, who may naturally emphasize control, peace, or correctness over flexibility. The goal is to help children develop both capacities in balance.

The Chen Family

Lisa (8) and David (9) support Marcus by:

- Validating protective instincts while encouraging sensitivity
- Supporting direct engagement with balanced restraint
- Allowing strong responses while maintaining connection
- Creating boundaries that protect yet remain flexible

The Patel Family

Priya (5) and Raj (7) support Maya by:

- Validating observation needs while encouraging engagement
- Supporting careful analysis while maintaining connection
- Allowing assessment time while building confidence
- Creating gentle encouragement that respects her pace

Understanding these personal ecologies of fear transforms how we view childhood behavior. What might look like defiance, withdrawal, or attention-seeking reveals itself as sophisticated territory mapping—each child's intelligent attempt to create safety in their world. Our role isn't to dismantle these territories but to support their healthy development while maintaining enough flexibility for growth.

As we explore shame in the next chapter, we'll discover how fear's protective wisdom interacts with our social emotions. We'll see how early experiences with fear influence our capacity for social engagement and how both emotions—fear and shame—work together in healthy development.

By understanding how children adapt to their parents' fear patterns, we help them develop:

- Trust in their protective instincts
- Confidence in their assessment abilities
- Flexibility in their response patterns
- Resilience in facing challenges

This understanding requires patience, presence, and commitment to our growth as parents. We often map new territories in our fear landscapes as we support our children's developing responses to fear. The reward is watching our children develop the confidence to explore while maintaining access to their natural protective wisdom.

Each parent's pattern offers different gifts and challenges in creating safety. By understanding these patterns early in life, we can support our children's healthy development while maintaining the flexibility that allows full engagement with life's possibilities.

Through this lens, childhood development reveals itself as a sophisticated adaptation process. Each child learns to navigate their world by mirroring and adapting to their parents' patterns of managing fear, creating complex landscapes of safety and challenge. Our role is to honor these adaptations while ensuring they remain flexible for growth.

As we transition from examining fear to exploring shame, reflect on how your Type's approach to protection and security influences your handling of social judgment and worth. Your relationship with fear—whether through vigilance, avoidance, or analysis—shapes how you create an environment for your child's social and emotional development. In the next chapter, we'll discover how your Type's characteristic approach to shame creates the atmosphere in which your child develops their sense of self in relation to others. We'll see how your patterns around worth and acceptance influence your child's emerging strategies for maintaining connection while developing identity.

Reflection

Take a few quiet moments to explore how your type's relationship with fear influences your child's developing safety strategies.

Your Fear Pattern

Consider your automatic responses to threat or uncertainty.

- How does your type typically manage fear?
- What strategies feel most natural to you?
- Where do you feel most challenged by uncertainty?

Your Child's Adaptations

Notice how your child may be adapting to your pattern.

- How do they respond when you're anxious?
- Where do you see your patterns reflected in their behavior?
- What aspects of your approach do they seem to mirror?

Remember: Your pattern isn't wrong—it's simply your way of creating safety. The key is understanding how it influences your child while maintaining enough flexibility for their authentic development.

What aspects of your type's relationship with fear need attention and care to better support your child's growing confidence?

Your Notes

Chapter 6

Shame—The Shape of Self

Children don't say, 'My parents are doing something wrong'; they say, 'Something is wrong with me.'
Dr. Gabor Maté

Five-year-old Sofia has just spilled her juice at the family dinner table. Her face flushes red, her shoulders hunch, her eyes drop to the floor, and her whole body seems to collapse inward. This isn't just embarrassment about making a mess; it's shame, one of the most potent forces shaping personality development in early childhood.

Across the table, her mother Ana (2) feels her shame response rising—memories of being called clumsy and careless as a child surge forth. Her Type Two pattern activates, urging her to quickly help and soothe, unconsciously passing on her shame pattern through overcompensation. Her husband Carlos's (4) pattern responds with heightened sensitivity to the emotional depth of the moment, his subtle reaction intensifying Sofia's experience of being seen in her vulnerability.

This moment, so common in early childhood, illuminates how shame operates as an isolated emotion and a profound architect of personality. Building on the foundations of acceptance, attachment, anger, and fear we've explored, shame emerges as the emotion that shapes our sense of self in relation to others.

Watch how Sofia's pattern formation emerges through daily interactions as she absorbs and mirrors her parents' approaches.

From Ana (2), she learns that:

- Worth comes through helping others
- Needs are something to be ashamed of
- Connection requires self-forgetting
- Being needed equals being loved

From Carlos (4), she absorbs that:

- Uniqueness protects from shame
- Emotional depth creates significance
- Being understood requires intensity
- Standing apart ensures connection

The Heart Triad (Types Two, Three, and Four) reveals how humans naturally relate to shame and self-image. Each type in this triad has a characteristic way of managing identity and worth. The patterns we see—particularly in Type Three's neutral position between hiding and displaying—illuminate something essential about how all personality structures manage this vital emotion.

Understanding how children adapt to their parents' shame patterns gives us unprecedented opportunities to support healthy development while maintaining flexibility in these vital patterns. Our role isn't to prevent shame or fix patterns but to understand how they form and support their healthy expression while maintaining enough flexibility for continued growth.

The Fundamental Nature of Shame

When three-year-old Sofia asks a question that makes adults uncomfortable, her response to their reaction shapes her future relationship with curiosity and self-expression. Her mother Ana (2) notices her impulse to smooth over the moment quickly but instead gets curious: "What made you wonder about that?" This approach maintains Sofia's natural inquisitiveness while helping her navigate social understanding.

Shame, unlike anger or fear, requires witnesses—real or imagined. Whether the eyes are physical or internalized, shame is fundamentally about being seen in a diminishing way. This truth reveals itself in the very physiology of shame: the downcast eyes, the averted face, the collapsed posture—all attempts to escape the gaze that seems to expose our unworthiness.

Watch how this dynamic plays out in two different family systems

The Smith Family Ecosystem (Types 3 and 1)

Lucas faces criticism during his school presentation. His automatic response mirrors Rachel's (3) pattern, immediately scanning the room for negative judgment as his body prepares to adjust his performance. Meanwhile, James's Type 1 influence manifests as Lucas internally critiquing his work against rigid standards of correctness. This isn't learned behavior but the fundamental nature of shame at work, teaching him that worth comes through successful performance and adherence to principles.Rachel's Type Three pattern intensifies this dynamic through:

- Quick attention to image management
- Subtle signals about acceptable presentation
- Unconscious emphasis on achievement
- Automatic reframing of "failure" as opportunity

The Rodriguez Family Dynamic (Types 2 and 4)

Sofia encounters social awkwardness at a birthday party. Her response reflects both Ana's (2) helping pattern and Carlos's (4) intensity:

- She immediately looks to help other children (Type Two adaptation)
- She creates elaborate emotional narratives about the experience (Type Four adaptation)
- Her body carries both patterns' shame responses
- Her coping strategies blend both parents' approaches

This shame response becomes internalized as the superego develops—that inner voice of judgment that carries the weight of all the eyes that have ever made us feel small, wrong, or unworthy. What begins as an external experience of being seen gradually becomes an internal state of constant self-surveillance. The child develops an inner eye that watches, judges, and shames.

Watch how this internalization unfolds.

Early Formation (2-4 years)

Emma's perfectionist responses already mirror Sarah's (1) pattern.

- Checking her work repeatedly before showing anyone
- Apologizing for minor imperfections
- Monitoring others' reactions vigilantly
- Creating elaborate systems for avoiding mistakes

Pattern Consolidation (4-6 years)

Maya's withdrawal strategies reflect Priya's (5) approach.

- Careful observation before engagement
- Strategic management of exposure
- Complex systems for avoiding shame
- Sophisticated protection of vulnerability

Understanding the fundamental nature of shame—its requirement for witnesses and its gradual internalization—transforms how we support our children's development. Each child's shame responses aren't just individual reactions but intelligent adaptations to their family's emotional ecosystem.

The Formation of Personality through Shame

The Enneagram's Heart Triad (Types Two, Three, and Four) reveals three fundamental ways children learn to manage shame and maintain connection. Each strategy emerges as an intelligent adaptation to early experiences, particularly around how their environment responds to their authentic self-expression and natural needs.

Watch how different parent-child pairs navigate this territory.

The Performance Strategy (Type Three Pattern)

Lucas, raised by Rachel (3) and James (1), learns early that acceptance depends on achievement and appearance. At five, he doesn't merely feel disappointed when he makes a small mistake during gymnastics class; he experiences a deep sense of personal failure. His natural joy in movement has become secondary to getting the moves "right."

This pattern develops when:

- Praise focuses primarily on achievement
- Love feels contingent on success
- Mistakes are met with disappointment
- The environment emphasizes image management

The child learns to:

- Scan for what others want
- Adapt quickly to expectations
- Hide authentic feelings
- Become what brings approval

Daily life reveals this pattern in subtle but significant moments. Watch Lucas practice his lines for the class play, his eyes constantly scanning the room for approval. Notice how quickly he shifts his behavior when he senses attention drifting away, already developing elaborate strategies to maintain his image of success.

The Complex Adaptation Pattern (Type Two and Four Influence)

Sofia, influenced by Ana (2) and Carlos (4), shows how children can absorb and mirror multiple patterns in managing shame. Her strategies reflect both parents' approaches:

From Ana's Type Two pattern:

- Securing connection through helping
- Managing shame through care for others
- Suppressing personal needs
- Finding worth through service

From Carlos's Type Four pattern:

- Creating unique identity as protection
- Managing shame through differentiation
- Developing emotional depth
- Finding significance through intensity

Watch how this complex mirroring unfolds in Sofia's daily life. During playground conflicts, she transforms ordinary interactions into elaborate emotional narratives, becoming both the mysterious character who stands apart (Type Four) and the caring helper who resolves everyone's feelings (Type Two).

The Knowledge Strategy (Type Five Pattern)

Maya, influenced by Priya's (5) pattern, develops a distinctive approach to managing shame through understanding and distance.

The pattern emerges when:

- Distance provides safety
- Knowledge equals protection
- Observation supersedes engagement
- Minimal presence feels secure

Maya learns to:

- Create intellectual territories
- Manage exposure through understanding
- Maintain protective distance
- Find safety in knowledge

Daily moments reveal this pattern as Maya develops increasingly sophisticated strategies for managing social interactions through careful observation and strategic engagement, mirroring her mother's approach to managing vulnerability through understanding.

Pattern Development through Stages

Early Formation (0-3 years)

Watch how different children begin absorbing their parents' shame patterns.

Emma with Sarah (1):

- Already checking her work carefully
- Showing early perfectionist tendencies
- Developing rigid standards
- Mirroring her mother's self-criticism

Lucas with Rachel (3):

- Scanning for performance opportunities
- Developing achievement focus
- Learning image management
- Mirroring success orientation

Pattern Consolidation (3-6 years)

Observe how these patterns become more sophisticated.

Sofia with Ana (2) and Carlos (4):

- Creating complex helping strategies
- Developing unique emotional expressions
- Blending care with differentiation
- Building elaborate identity structures

Maya with Priya (5):

- Establishing knowledge territories
- Creating observation posts
- Developing resource protection

- Building safety through understanding

Through these stages, children aren't just developing individual responses to shame; they're absorbing and adapting to their parents' established patterns while creating unique strategies for managing this powerful emotion.

Family Systems and Shame Transmission

Shame patterns pass through generations and interact within family systems. Watch how different family ecosystems manage and transmit shame.

The Heart Center Ecosystem (Types 2 and 4)

Ana (2) and Carlos (4) (Rodriguez family) create an atmosphere where shame interweaves with emotional intensity and connection. Their combined patterns create a complex environment where Sofia learns to navigate worth by helping and being unique.

Their ecosystem develops through:

- Emotional intensity signifying importance
- Connection protecting from shame
- Helping securing worth
- Uniqueness ensuring significance

Sofia learns to:

- Amplify emotional experiences
- Maintain special status through helping
- Care for others' feelings deeply
- Create meaningful narratives about herself

Daily life reveals this complex pattern through Sofia's rich emotional storytelling. Watch how she navigates increasingly complex relationship dynamics, weaving elaborate patterns of helping others into her interactions. She's already developing sophisticated ways of making meaning from everyday experiences, turning simple moments into opportunities for emotional connection and significance.

The Head Center Ecosystem (Types 5 and 7)

Priya (5) and Raj (7) (Patel family) establish an environment where shame management occurs through knowledge and reframing. Their combined influence creates a unique atmosphere where Maya learns to handle shame through understanding and possibility-seeking.

Their system operates through:

- Knowledge providing protection
- Options offering escape
- Understanding creating safety
- Reframing maintaining hope

Maya develops:

- Sophisticated observation strategies
- Multiple ways of avoiding exposure
- Complex understanding systems
- Quick reframing abilities

Watch how this manifests in Maya's daily life. During social challenges, she combines careful observation with quick movement to new possibilities, reflecting both parents' strategies for managing vulnerability.

The Body Center Ecosystem (Types 8 and 9)

Lisa (8) and David (9) (Chen family) create an environment where shame management occurs through strength and peace-making. Their contrasting patterns establish a dynamic where Marcus learns to handle shame through both power and harmony.

Their system functions through:

- Strength providing protection
- Peace maintaining connection
- Power ensuring safety

- Harmony avoiding shame

Marcus learns to:

- Assert strength carefully
- Navigate conflict smoothly
- Balance power with peace
- Maintain connection through challenge

Daily interactions reveal this balance as Marcus develops increasingly nuanced ways of being strong while maintaining harmony, integrating both parents' approaches to managing vulnerability.

Working with Family Shame Patterns

Different family systems require different approaches to supporting healthy shame development.

Heart Center Families

When working with emotional intensity:

- Support authentic feeling without amplification
- Allow connection without enmeshment
- Validate experience without drama
- Maintain boundaries while staying connected

Head Center Families

When managing through knowledge:

- Support understanding without withdrawal
- Allow observation while maintaining engagement
- Validate thinking without disconnection
- Create safety through balanced presence

Body Center Families

When handling through action:

- Support strength without overwhelming
- Allow peace without avoidance
- Validate power while maintaining connection
- Create safety through balanced assertion

The key to working with these patterns lies not in preventing shame but in maintaining enough flexibility that shame can serve its developmental purpose without becoming rigid or destructive. This requires parents to:

- Recognize their inherited shame patterns
- Work consciously with triggered responses
- Support children's natural development
- Maintain connection through shame experiences

Understanding how shame patterns operate in family systems can help us create environments that support healthy development while maintaining flexibility for continued growth. This isn't about eliminating shame but helping children develop resilient ways of managing this fundamental human emotion.

Supporting Your Child through Shame

Understanding shame's role in personality development helps us better support our children through shame experiences. The goal isn't to prevent shame—that's neither possible nor desirable—but to help children maintain flexibility in responding to it.

Our shame patterns profoundly influence how we respond to our children's shame experiences. Each type in the Heart Triad carries specific blind spots and gifts in parenting through shame moments.

Working with Different Parent Patterns

Type Two Parents (Like Ana)

Watch Ana's pattern emerge when Sofia faces social rejection.

Without awareness, Ana might:

- Absorb Sofia's shame as her own
- Rush to fix the social situation
- Over-help to ease the pain
- Miss opportunities for growth

Through conscious work, Ana learns to:

- Notice her helping impulse without acting
- Allow natural social processing
- Support without taking over
- Maintain connection without merging

Type Three Parents (Like Rachel)

Observe Rachel's pattern when Lucas struggles with a presentation.

Without awareness, Rachel might:

- Jump to performance coaching
- Focus on image recovery
- Push for quick success
- Miss the emotional experience

Through conscious work, Rachel practices:

- Feeling her achievement anxiety arise
- Staying present with the struggle
- Supporting authentic expression
- Maintaining connection beyond performance

Type Four Parents (Like Carlos)

Watch Carlos's pattern activate when Sofia feels misunderstood.

Without awareness, Carlos might:

- Amplify the emotional drama
- Deepen the sense of being different
- Intensify the experience of rejection
- Miss opportunities for simple connection

Through development, Carlos learns to:

- Notice his intensifying impulse
- Stay grounded in the present moment
- Support without dramatizing
- Maintain balanced emotional presence

Supporting Different Shame Responses

The Performance-Sensitive Child

When Lucas freezes after a mistake, Rachel (3) learns to:

Provide Immediate Support:

- Maintain steady presence
- Allow natural processing
- Offer simple acknowledgment
- Create space for recovery

Develop Long-term Strategies:

- Support worth beyond achievement
- Build genuine self-acceptance
- Create safety for mistakes
- Maintain unconditional connection

The Connection-Sensitive Child

When Sofia experiences social shame, Ana (2) practices:

Immediate Response:

- Stay present without fixing
- Allow natural emotional flow
- Support without overwhelming
- Maintain gentle presence

Long-term Development:

- Build healthy boundaries
- Support authentic needs
- Create balanced helping
- Maintain self-connection

The Observation-Sensitive Child

When Maya encounters exposure shame, Priya (5) works to:

Immediate Support:

- Respect withdrawal needs
- Allow natural processing
- Support gentle engagement
- Maintain careful presence

Long-term Growth:

- Build balanced connection
- Support measured exposure
- Create safe engagement
- Maintain flexible boundaries

Integration in Daily Life

Different family systems require different approaches to integrating shame work:

The Connor Family Approach (Types 1 and 6)

Sarah (1) and Michael (6) support Emma through:

- Clear but flexible boundaries
- Structured emotional processing
- Balanced perfectionist tendencies
- Maintained loving presence

The Patel Family Method (Types 5 and 7)

Priya (5) and Raj (7) help Maya by:

- Respecting observation needs
- Supporting gradual engagement
- Balancing withdrawal and connection
- Maintaining steady presence

The Chen Family Practice (Types 8 and 9)

Lisa (8) and David (9) work with Marcus through:

- Protected emotional expression
- Balanced strength and vulnerability
- Supporting authentic power
- Maintaining steady containment

The Rodriguez Family Approach (Types 2 and 4)

Ana (2) and Carlos (4) support Sofia by:

- Balancing helping with space

- Supporting emotional depth without drama
- Allowing authentic needs
- Maintaining connection without merging

The Smith Family Method (Types 1 and 3)

Rachel (3) and James (1) help Lucas through:

- Separating worth from achievement
- Supporting authenticity beyond image
- Balancing structure with expression
- Maintaining connection beyond performance

We create conditions for genuine growth and resilience through conscious engagement with our patterns while supporting our children's natural development. The goal isn't to eliminate shame but to help our children develop flexible, healthy ways of managing this fundamental human emotion.

Integration and Moving Forward

Your child's relationship with shame will continue to evolve. Your presence, acceptance, and conscious engagement create the foundation for lifelong emotional health and resilience. Understanding how shame shapes personality development while maintaining flexibility in our responses helps our children develop the capacity to handle life's challenges with authenticity and grace.

The Developmental Journey

Foundation Years (0-3)

Watch how conscious acceptance supports early development.

The Rodriguez Family learns to:

- Support Sofia's authentic expression
- Maintain connection through difficulty
- Allow natural emotional processing

- Build trust in relationship

Ana (2) works with her helping pattern by:

- Noticing the urge to fix or rescue
- Staying present with discomfort
- Supporting natural development
- Maintaining balanced connection

Patterning Years (3-6)

Observe how acceptance shapes emerging patterns:

The Smith Family helps Lucas by:

- Supporting genuine self-expression
- Maintaining worth beyond achievement
- Allowing natural development
- Building secure connection

Rachel (3) develops through:

- Working with performance anxiety
- Staying present with struggle
- Supporting authentic being
- Maintaining unconditional presence

Building Long-Term Resilience

True integration happens when children can:

- Experience shame without being overwhelmed
- Maintain connection during difficult emotions
- Recover naturally from shame experiences
- Access multiple response options

The goal is to support the development of humans who can:

- Experience shame without being defined by it
- Maintain connection through difficult emotions
- Recover naturally from moments of disconnection
- Navigate social belonging while staying authentic

This is the path toward true emotional resilience—not the absence of shame, but the ability to move through it with wisdom, courage, and authentic presence. Each interaction becomes an opportunity to help our children develop a healthier relationship with being seen, being human, and being themselves in all their beautiful imperfections.

Supporting Ongoing Development

Different family systems find unique ways of supporting this integration:

The Heart Center Approach

Ana (2) and Carlos (4) support Sofia through:

- Balanced emotional engagement
- Authentic self-expression
- Natural relationship development
- Maintained loving presence

The Head Center Method

Priya (5) and Raj (7) help Maya by:

- Respecting processing needs
- Supporting gradual engagement
- Balancing understanding with experience
- Maintaining steady connection

The Body Center Practice

Lisa (8) and David (9) work with Marcus through:

- Integrated strength and gentleness
- Balanced power and peace
- Natural boundary development
- Maintained protective presence

Your growing understanding of your pattern creates space for you and your child to unfold more authentically. Each challenging moment offers an opportunity for mutual growth and deeper connection.

This sacred dance of development transforms both parent and child. As we learn to hold our children's shame experiences with wisdom and compassion, we create a container of love that allows their unique essence to flourish. And in that space of conscious witnessing, we, too, are changed, growing into more spacious and authentic versions of ourselves.

Shifting from our exploration of shame to examining the superego, consider how your Type's approach to social judgment and worth influences your inner critic's development and expression. Your particular relationship with shame—whether through performance, helping, or differentiation—shapes the internal voices that your child internalizes through daily interactions with you. In the next chapter, we'll discover how your Type's characteristic superego patterns become transmitted to your child, creating their inner guidance system. We'll see how your relationship with self-judgment influences your child's emerging relationship with themselves.

Reflection

Take a few quiet moments to explore your relationship with shame, both in your history and parenting. This powerful emotion shapes how we experience being seen and learn to see ourselves.

Your Pattern's Influence

Consider your automatic responses to shame.

- What happens in your body when shame arises?
- How does your type typically manage this emotion?
- Where do you feel most challenged by your child's shame?
- What helps you stay present with this force?

The Living Laboratory

Consider a recent shame moment with your child.

- What happened in your body?
- How did your pattern want to respond?
- Where did you find flexibility?
- What helped you stay present?

Remember: Shame serves vital developmental purposes. Your child needs to experience your balanced relationship with this emotion to develop their healthy sense of worth.

Take time to write about what support your pattern needs to hold space for shame in your parenting.

Your Notes

Chapter 7

The Superego—When Emotions Turn Against the Self

When a child turns anger inward, the superego is born.

As we explore the superego, we'll discover how the primary emotions become enlisted in patterns of self-regulation and how these patterns pass from one generation to the next. We'll see how early experiences with acceptance, attachment, anger, fear, and shame become organized into an internal system of self-judgment and control.

Six-year-old Emma sits at her desk, tears welling up as she erases her drawing for the third time. Her mother, Sarah (1), watches from the doorway, her body tense with familiar anxiety. In this simple moment, we can see the inheritance of the superego at work—how patterns of self-judgment pass through generations.

Watch as the scene unfolds, revealing how the primary emotions become enlisted in self-regulation.

Fear emerges first: Emma's hand hesitates above the paper, her body tense with anticipation of making another mistake. This isn't just performance anxiety; it's her mother's unexamined relationship with imperfection mirrored in Emma's nervous system.

Then anger turns inward: "I'm so stupid," she whispers, pressing the eraser harder against the paper. This self-directed aggression echoes Sarah's internal battles with perfectionism, which she has now unconsciously transmitted to her daughter.

Finally, shame completes the cycle: Emma's shoulders hunch as she glances anxiously at her previous drawings. Her whole body carries the message that she is fundamentally flawed—a belief inherited through thousands of subtle interactions with her family's patterns of self-judgment.

But watch what happens next. Sarah feels her Type One pattern activate, urging her to fix and improve the situation. "Don't be so hard on yourself!" she says, her voice carrying its tightness—the same tone her mother used decades ago. When she adds,

"Look how well you did on the other parts!" she unconsciously transmits the message that there is something to judge, fix, and improve.

This scene—repeated countless times in different ways throughout childhood—illuminates how the superego develops. By age six, a child's inner critic is primarily formed, built from thousands of such moments where they internalize their parents' words and their entire relationship with themselves.

Understanding this process gives us unprecedented opportunities to support healthy development while maintaining flexibility in these vital patterns. Our role isn't to prevent the superego from forming—that's neither possible nor desirable—but to understand how it develops and support its healthy expression while maintaining enough flexibility for continued growth.

The Inheritance of Inner Voices

The Enneagram helps us recognize how superego patterns transmit from generation to generation. Watch three different parent-child pairs working on projects, each revealing how distinct patterns of self-judgment pass through generations.

The Heart Center Patterns

The Helping Pattern (Type Two)

Sofia watches Ana (2) during family gatherings, absorbing her mother's subtle signals about worth and connection. Without conscious awareness, Ana transmits her pattern through:

- Attentive responses to others' needs
- Subtle praise for helpfulness
- Unconscious dismissal of personal wants
- Automatic prioritizing of relationships

Sofia absorbs these messages, developing:

- Vigilant monitoring of others' feelings
- Worth through being needed
- Complex helping strategies

- Sophisticated relationship management

Daily life reveals this inherited pattern as Sofia frequently checks if others need anything before expressing her desires. Notice how she offers to help her playmates before joining activities, already developing elaborate strategies to secure connection through indispensability.

The Performance Pattern (Type Three)

Watch Lucas during homework time, Rachel (3) hovering nearby. His subtle body tension mirrors his mother's unresolved relationship with achievement. Without conscious awareness, Rachel transmits her pattern through:

- Quick attention to performance details
- Subtle signals about acceptable standards
- Unconscious emphasis on image
- Automatic reframing of "failure"

Lucas absorbs these messages, developing:

- Constant self-evaluation
- Worth through achievement
- Complex success strategies
- Sophisticated image management

Daily life reveals this inherited pattern as Lucas practices his lines for a school play, his eyes constantly scanning the room for approval. Notice how quickly he shifts his behavior when he senses attention drifting away, already developing elaborate strategies to maintain his image of success.

The Uniqueness Pattern (Type Four)

Observe Sofia with Carlos (4) during creative activities, absorbing her father's relationship with significance and depth. Without conscious awareness, Carlos transmits his pattern through:

- Special attention to unique qualities

- Subtle emphasis on emotional depth
- Unconscious dramatization of experiences
- Automatic focus on what's missing

Sofia absorbs these messages, developing:

- Heightened sense of uniqueness
- Worth through depth and difference
- Complex emotional narratives
- Sophisticated identity cultivation

Daily life reveals this inherited pattern as Sofia transforms ordinary experiences into meaningful moments. Watch how she creates elaborate stories about simple events, already developing sophisticated strategies to maintain specialness through emotional significance.

The Head Center Patterns

The Observer Pattern (Type Five)

Priya's (5) relationship with knowledge and distance becomes apparent in Maya's careful approach to experiences. Watch their patterns interweave.

Without awareness, Priya might:

- Transmit disconnection through analysis
- Model detached observation
- Pass on resource conservation
- Share intellectual defenses

Through conscious work, she learns to:

- Notice her withdrawal impulse
- Recognize inherited distance patterns
- Stay present with engagement

- Support balanced connection

Maya gradually internalizes:

- Sophisticated observation systems
- Complex knowledge territories
- Elaborate resource management
- Advanced emotional distancing

The Security Pattern (Type Six)

Michael's (6) complex relationship with authority and safety becomes evident in Emma's emerging self-talk. Watch their patterns interweave.

Without awareness, Michael might:

- Transmit anxiety about uncertainty
- Model constant checking behavior
- Pass on authority conflicts
- Share catastrophic thinking

Through conscious work, he learns to:

- Notice his scanning impulse
- Recognize inherited doubt patterns
- Stay present with uncertainty
- Support balanced assessment

Emma gradually internalizes:

- Sophisticated checking systems
- Complex safety strategies
- Elaborate preparation routines
- Advanced threat assessment

The Option Pattern (Type Seven)

Raj's (7) relationship with possibilities and avoidance becomes visible in Maya's approach to difficulty. Watch their patterns interweave.

Without awareness, Raj might:

- Transmit discomfort with limitation
- Model constant reframing
- Pass on pain avoidance
- Share scattered attention

Through conscious work, he learns to:

- Notice his escape impulse
- Recognize inherited avoidance patterns
- Stay present with discomfort
- Support balanced engagement

Maya gradually internalizes:

- Sophisticated reframing systems
- Complex option generation
- Elaborate planning strategies
- Advanced discomfort avoidance

The Body Center Patterns

The Direct Force Pattern (Type Eight)

Lisa's (8) relationship with power and protection becomes evident in Marcus's approach to boundaries. Watch their patterns interweave.

Without awareness, Lisa might:

- Transmit intensity around control

- Model forceful assertion
- Pass on vulnerability avoidance
- Share black-and-white thinking

Through conscious work, she learns to:

- Notice her control impulse
- Recognize inherited force patterns
- Stay present with vulnerability
- Support balanced strength

Marcus gradually internalizes:

- Sophisticated protection systems
- Complex power strategies
- Elaborate boundary setting
- Advanced vulnerability management

The Peaceful Merger Pattern (Type Nine)

David's (9) relationship with conflict and peace becomes visible in Marcus's approach to tension. Watch their patterns interweave.

Without awareness, David might:

- Transmit discomfort with conflict
- Model self-forgetting
- Pass on indirect communication
- Share numbing strategies

Through conscious work, he learns to:

- Notice his merging impulse
- Recognize inherited avoidance patterns

- Stay present with discomfort
- Support balanced assertion

Marcus gradually internalizes:

- Sophisticated harmony systems
- Complex conflict avoidance
- Elaborate peace-making strategies
- Advanced self-forgetting

The Perfectionist Pattern (Type One)

Sarah's (1) relationship with inner criticism becomes visible in Emma's artwork sessions. Watch their patterns interweave.

Without awareness, Sarah might:

- Transmit subtle signals about "rightness"
- Model constant self-improvement
- Show tension around imperfection
- Demonstrate rigid self-control

Through development, she learns to:

- Notice her perfecting impulse
- Recognize inherited standards
- Stay present with "mistakes"
- Support natural expression

Emma absorbs:

- Elaborate checking systems
- Complex standards for behavior
- Sophisticated self-monitoring

- Advanced criticism patterns

Consider this common scenario: A Type One father tries to help his son be "less perfectionistic" about homework. But beneath his helpful suggestions lurks his unexamined relationship with mistakes. His attempts at assistance transmit his superego's demands, now doubled in intensity because they're masked as help.

Watch him realize this during one homework session. As he starts to say, "Maybe you should…" he suddenly feels the familiar tightness in his chest—the same tension he felt at his childhood desk, trying to make everything perfect. In this moment of awareness, he pauses, takes a breath, and feels his old pattern. Only then can he truly be present with his son's experience rather than unconsciously transmitting his perfectionistic tendencies.

This is how inner voices pass through generations—not just through words but bodies, tones, gestures, and unconscious patterns. Each Type's particular flavor of self-judgment becomes part of the child's developing superego structure unless conscious awareness creates space for different possibilities.

The goal isn't to prevent these voices from forming. They serve vital developmental purposes. Instead, we aim to support their healthy expression while maintaining enough flexibility that they can continue evolving throughout life.

How Patterns Become Fixed

Watch how these patterns become internalized through daily interactions across different developmental stages. What appears as natural development is a subtle process of internalizing family patterns.

Early Signs of Pattern Formation (0-2 years)

At eight months, Maya is in her high chair, face scrunching as Priya (5) offers pureed peas. Without hesitation, she turns her head away, her small hand pushing at the spoon. Her body arches in protest—a clear "No!" expressed through movement. This is anger in its purest form—a life force expressing preference and boundary.

But notice what happens next. Carrying her unexamined discomfort with confrontation, Priya quickly shifts to distraction: "Look at the birdie!" Maya's natural emotion meets her mother's pattern in this subtle moment. While Maya won't yet internalize this response, her nervous system is already learning: strong feelings lead to disconnection.

Key Understanding:

- Natural emotions are pure and functional
- Family patterns influence self-judgment
- Nervous system creates early associations
- Foundation for later internalization forms

Pattern Formation Begins (2-4 years)

Watch three-year-old Sofia before her fallen block tower. First comes pure frustration—hands clenching, face reddening. But notice what happens next. Ana (2) subtly tenses. Before she can speak, Sofia says, "I'll help someone else build instead." This isn't just frustration redirecting. It's Sofia absorbing her mother's pattern of managing complicated feelings through helping others.

The process reveals itself through:

- Early self-talk emerging
- Physical responses mirroring parents
- Emotional strategies developing
- Coping patterns forming

Critical Period (4-6 years)

By this stage, we see how different children consolidate their inherited patterns.

Emma with Sarah (1):

- Perfectionist responses become automatic
- Self-criticism grows sophisticated
- Standards become internalized
- Inner judge takes shape

Lucas under Rachel's (3) influence:

- Achievement becomes central to identity
- Performance patterns solidify
- Image management becomes automatic
- Success strategies become habitual

Maya with Priya's (5) impact:

- Knowledge-seeking becomes security
- Observation patterns stabilize
- Distance-management becomes routine
- Understanding becomes primary safety

These patterns are primarily consolidated by age six, though not yet completely rigid. The superego structure is established, but there's still flexibility if parents can consciously recognize and work with their patterns.

Daily Life under the Inner Critic

Watch how these internalized patterns play out in everyday moments, shaping both children's experiences and parents' responses.

Morning Routines

Six-year-old Emma getting dressed for school:

- Tries on multiple outfits seeking "perfection"
- Worries about what others will think
- Criticizes herself for taking too long
- Seeks constant reassurance from Sarah (1)

Sarah notices her Type One pattern activating:

- Feels tension around time management
- Experiences urge to correct choices

- Struggles between efficiency and acceptance
- Unconsciously transmits perfectionism

Academic Learning

Lucas preparing for a presentation:

- Rehearses excessively
- Focuses on performance over content
- Monitors for possible failure
- Seeks approval from Rachel (3)

Rachel works with her Type Three influence:

- Emphasizes appearance and delivery
- Projects success anxiety
- Focuses on achievement
- Promotes image management

Understanding how these patterns become fixed gives us unprecedented opportunities to support healthy development while maintaining flexibility. Our role isn't to prevent pattern formation but to help ensure patterns remain adaptable enough for continued growth.

Breaking the Pattern

Understanding how superego patterns transmit transforms how we approach supporting children's development. No amount of positive parenting techniques or behavioral strategies can prevent this transmission if parents haven't done their deep work.

The Illusion of Strategy

Watch what happens when parents try using techniques without addressing their patterns.

Sarah (1) with Emma:

The parenting book advised, "Use 'I' statements." So Sarah says, "I see how hard you're trying," but her voice still carries that tight anxiety about performance. Emma's body responds not to the carefully crafted words but to the unprocessed tension in her mother's tone.

Rachel (3) with Lucas:

The workshop taught "Validate feelings." So Rachel offers, "It's okay to feel frustrated," but her quick, nervous energy betrays her discomfort with missing the mark. Lucas absorbs not the verbal permission but the bodily message that difficult feelings need to be quickly managed.

Ana (2) with Sofia:

The teacher suggested, "Create growth mindset moments." Ana says, "Mistakes help us learn," but her subtle flinch when Sofia's crayon slips reveals a deeper truth about her unhealed relationship with error.

The Real Work

True change requires parents to face what they'd rather avoid.

- Their harsh inner critic
- Childhood wounds around worth
- Unprocessed emotional patterns
- Inherited family beliefs

Consider these transformative moments.

Sarah's Journey

When Emma struggles with perfectionism in art class, Sarah (1):

- Notices her tension rising
- Feels the familiar tightness in her chest
- Recognizes her childhood pattern

- Chooses to stay present without fixing

Rachel's Growth

As Lucas obsesses over his presentation, Rachel (3):

- Feels her achievement anxiety activate
- Recognizes her worth-through-success equation
- Connects with her childhood pressure
- Chooses to value being over doing

Priya's Development

When Maya withdraws from social situations, Priya (5):

- Notices her withdrawal impulse
- Recognizes her safety-through-distance pattern
- Connects with her childhood isolation
- Chooses to stay engaged while respecting boundaries

Supporting Development through Conscious Presence

Let's return to Emma at her desk, erasing her drawing repeatedly. The typical parenting response might be to reach for strategies: positive reinforcement, growth mindset statements, distraction techniques. But watch what happens when Sarah (1) approaches differently, having done her deep work with perfectionism.

She first feels her body's response to Emma's distress. Notices her impulse to fix, to soothe, to make better. Recognizes these as echoes of her own unmet childhood needs. Then, instead of acting from these patterns, she sits quietly beside Emma. "Drawing brings up lots of feelings," she says softly, her presence arising not from technique but from her inner work.

The Difference Conscious Work Makes

Watch these contrasting moments.

Without Inner Work

A Type One father sees his son struggling with homework. His unexamined perfectionism activates, and despite his best intentions, his "help" carries the tension of his unresolved patterns. His suggestions, though technically sound, transmit his anxiety about mistakes.

With Inner Work

Having faced his relationship with perfectionism, the same father feels the familiar tightness arise. He pauses, breathes, notices. His presence with his son now comes from a place of worked-through understanding rather than an unconscious pattern.

Let's return one final time to Emma at her desk, tears welling up as she erases her drawing. But now we can see the full depth of this moment—not just a child struggling with perfectionism, but the meeting point of generations. In her small body lives her mother's unresolved relationship with mistakes, her father's anxious pursuit of approval, her grandmother's rigid standards, and her grandfather's fear of inadequacy. The superego she's forming will carry all these voices unless her parents do the deep work of facing their inheritance.

Through understanding how these patterns form and consciously working with their development, we help our children build internal structures that guide rather than constrain, protect rather than imprison, and support rather than criticize.

As we move from examining the superego to exploring curiosity, notice how your Type's inner critic influences your openness to wonder and not-knowing. Your particular relationship with self-judgment—whether through perfectionism, achievement-focus, or analysis—shapes how you create an environment for your child's natural exploration. In the next chapter, we'll discover how your Type's characteristic approach to curiosity creates the space in which your child develops their relationship with learning and discovery. We'll see how your patterns around knowing and understanding influence your child's emerging strategies for engaging with their world.

Reflection

Take a few quiet moments to explore the voices within your superego, not as "your" voice but as an inheritance of internalized others. This delicate work requires slowing down enough to really listen and discriminate.

Tracing the Lineage

Sit quietly and listen to your inner critical voice.

- What are its familiar phrases and tones?
- Who does it sound like—a parent, teacher, culture?
- Where did these standards originate?
- What emotion accompanies this voice?

The Transmission Chain

Consider how these inherited voices might now speak through you.

- What phrases do you catch yourself saying to your child?
- Whose voice are you really hearing in those moments?
- What familiar tones or messages emerge under stress?
- How might your child internalize these voices?

Remember: Your inner critic isn't your authentic voice; it's a tapestry of internalized others woven through generations. Recognizing these voices as not-self creates space for your authentic voice to emerge.

Your Notes

Chapter 8

Curiosity—The Flame of Being

The question is not what you look at, but what you see.
Henry David Thoreau

As we explore curiosity, we'll discover how this vital force interacts with our patterns, offering a path for maintaining flexibility rather than rigidity. We'll see how early experiences with acceptance, attachment, anger, fear, and shame influence our relationship with wonder and how curiosity can keep these patterns adaptable throughout life.

Picture this: Four-year-old Maya discovers a fallen leaf on her way to preschool. She stops, crouches down, and examines it with complete absorption. "Look!" she exclaims to her mother, "It has tiny lines like rivers!" Her mother Priya (5) feels the familiar tension between honoring her daughter's wonder and maintaining the schedule. Now, she faces a choice that will subtly shape Maya's relationship with curiosity and potentially her growth.

Watch what happens next. Priya feels her pattern activate—the familiar tightness that says time must be managed, energy preserved, and demands controlled. But instead of immediately hurrying Maya along, she pauses and gets curious about her reaction. "What's making me so uncomfortable with this delay?" This simple moment of wondering about her pattern creates space for her growth and for Maya's natural exploration.

This moment, repeated countless times in different ways throughout childhood, illuminates the dual opportunity before us. First, we support our children's natural curiosity during the early years before patterns become fixed. Second, we must use curiosity to examine and soften our patterns, creating more space for genuine presence with our children.

Throughout this book, we've explored how personality patterns emerge and become fixed.

- Through the fundamental need for acceptance
- Within the web of early attachment
- Through the expression of vital anger
- In response to protective fear
- Shaped by social shame
- Consolidated in the superego

Now we discover how curiosity offers a path through these patterns, not to eliminate them but to maintain their flexibility and wisdom while supporting growth. Curiosity isn't just a charming quality of childhood; it's the fundamental force that can keep patterns flexible rather than rigid.

Watch how different parent patterns influence their children's relationship with wonder.

Maya with Priya (5):

- Natural observation meets analytical distance
- Wonder encounters energy management
- Exploration faces withdrawal patterns
- Discovery meets knowledge-seeking

Emma with Sarah (1):

- Spontaneous exploration meets structure needs
- Messy investigation encounters order patterns
- Creative expression faces perfectionist tendencies
- Natural wonder meets improvement impulses

By understanding how curiosity interacts with our patterns, we gain unprecedented opportunities to support our children's natural wonder and growth. Our role isn't to maintain childlike curiosity forever—that's neither possible nor desirable—but to help ensure that wonder can continue serving development throughout life.

The Dance of Discovery

Watch eleven-month-old Sofia encountering a new texture. Her whole body becomes involved in the investigation: fingers probe, mouth tastes, eyes study intently. This isn't just play; it's her nervous system building crucial neural pathways through direct sensory engagement with her world. Her mother Ana (2) feels the familiar urge to interrupt: "Don't put that in your mouth!" But today, something different happens. She notices her anxiety and gets curious about it. "What am I afraid of here?" This moment of self-reflection creates space for Sofia's natural exploration to unfold safely.

Curiosity's Connection to Primary Emotions

Curiosity intertwines deeply with the three primary emotions we've explored, each interaction shaping how children learn to engage with their world.

Curiosity and Anger

When three-year-old Marcus's block tower falls, his initial frustration can shut down exploration or fuel deeper investigation. His response often depends on how his environment handles the intersection of anger and curiosity. Lisa (8) felt her impulse to jump in with solutions but instead asked, "What made it fall? What if we try it differently?" This transforms anger's energy into curiosity's fuel.

Anger supports curiosity by:

- Providing energy for persistence
- Highlighting what matters to us
- Motivating problem-solving
- Protecting awe

Watch how Marcus uses this energy to test different building approaches, experimenting with various strategies. His mother's comfort with strength allows him to stay engaged through frustration, transforming potential anger into determined exploration.

Curiosity and Fear

See six-year-old Emma approaching a new playground structure. Her natural curiosity pulls her toward exploration, while fear creates a necessary pause for assessment. Sarah (1) feels her pattern urging caution. But instead of saying, "Be careful," she asks, "What do you notice about the climb?" This interaction between curiosity and fear isn't a problem to solve but a dynamic to support.

Fear enhances curiosity through:

- Creating appropriate caution
- Supporting careful observation
- Encouraging thorough investigation
- Protecting boundaries

Emma demonstrates this balance by methodically testing each step, ensuring safe progress while maintaining her exploratory drive. Her mother's work with perfectionism allows space for both caution and adventure.

Curiosity and Shame

When four-year-old Sofia asks a question that makes adults uncomfortable, her response to their reaction shapes her future relationship with curiosity. Ana (2) notices her impulse to smooth over the moment quickly but instead gets curious: "What made you wonder about that?" This approach maintains Sofia's natural inquisitiveness while helping her navigate social understanding.

Curiosity transforms shame by:

- Maintaining connection during mistakes
- Celebrating unusual questions
- Supporting recovery after social missteps
- Protecting authentic interest

Watch Sofia develop as she gains confidence in asking questions and embraces curiosity without hesitation. Her parents' ability to stay present with discomfort allows her natural wonder to flourish, even in socially challenging moments.

By understanding these interactions between curiosity and primary emotions, we can better support our children's natural exploration while helping them maintain flexible responses to life's challenges. Each parent's pattern offers different opportunities and challenges in this dance of discovery.

Type Five Parents (Like Priya)

Natural gifts:

- Value understanding deeply
- Support careful observation
- Respect investigation time
- Create space for processing

Growth edges:

- Maintaining emotional presence
- Engaging with messy exploration
- Supporting physical discovery
- Allowing energetic expression

Type One Parents (Like Sarah)

Natural gifts:

- Value thorough exploration
- Support structured investigation
- Respect careful progress
- Create clear learning paths

Growth edges:

- Allowing messy discovery
- Supporting spontaneous exploration
- Maintaining flexible boundaries

- Embracing uncertain outcomes

Type Two Parents (Like Ana)

Natural gifts:

- Value emotional discovery
- Support relational exploration
- Respect personal connections
- Create nurturing learning environments

Growth edges:

- Allowing independent investigation
- Supporting solitary exploration
- Maintaining appropriate distance
- Embracing self-directed curiosity

Type Three Parents (Like Rachel)

Natural gifts:

- Value efficient learning
- Support goal-oriented exploration
- Respect achievement milestones
- Create engaging learning opportunities

Growth edges:

- Allowing unproductive curiosity
- Supporting process over outcomes
- Maintaining patience with meandering exploration
- Embracing curiosity without purpose

Type Four Parents (Like Carlos)

Natural gifts:

- Value unique discoveries
- Support emotional depth in exploration
- Respect individual expression
- Create meaningful learning experiences

Growth edges:

- Allowing ordinary curiosity
- Supporting practical exploration
- Maintaining consistent engagement
- Embracing simple discoveries

Type Six Parents (Like Michael)

Natural gifts:

- Value careful investigation
- Support thorough questioning
- Respect safety in exploration
- Create secure learning environments

Growth edges:

- Allowing uncertain exploration
- Supporting risk in discovery
- Maintaining trust in the process
- Embracing ambiguous findings

Type Seven Parents (Like Raj)

Natural gifts:

- Value enthusiastic exploration
- Support diverse investigations
- Respect multiple interests
- Create exciting learning environments

Growth edges:

- Allowing focused, sustained curiosity
- Supporting depth over breadth
- Maintaining presence with difficulties
- Embracing slower, methodical exploration

Type Eight Parents (Like Lisa)

Natural gifts:

- Value bold exploration
- Support confident investigation
- Respect independence in discovery
- Create empowering learning environments

Growth edges:

- Allowing tentative curiosity
- Supporting gentle exploration
- Maintaining patience with uncertainty
- Embracing subtle discoveries

Type Nine Parents (Like David)

Natural gifts:

- Value inclusive exploration
- Support harmonious investigation
- Respect natural learning rhythms
- Create comfortable discovery environments

Growth edges:

- Allowing challenging curiosity
- Supporting focused exploration
- Maintaining consistent engagement
- Embracing disruptive discoveries

This dance between parent patterns and children's natural curiosity shapes how wonder and exploration develop. Our role isn't to maintain perpetual childlike curiosity but to support its evolution into a lifelong tool for growth and discovery.

The Development of Curiosity

The Foundation Years (0-3): Raw Wonder

During these foundational years, curiosity is primarily expressed through sensory and physical exploration. Watch eleven-month-old Maya encounter different textures. Her whole body becomes involved in the investigation: fingers probe, mouth tastes, eyes study intently. This isn't just play; it's her nervous system building crucial neural pathways through direct sensory engagement with her world.

Key manifestations during this period include:

- Mouthing and handling everything within reach
- Intense observation of faces and expressions
- Physical experimentation with cause and effect
- Full-body engagement with new experiences

Watch how different parent patterns interact with this stage.

Type One Parents like Sarah might struggle with the mess and disorder of early exploration:

- Wanting to keep things clean and orderly
- Feeling uncomfortable with "inappropriate" exploration
- Trying to direct play into "proper" channels

But when they get curious about their discomfort, they ponder:

- What's making me so anxious about this mess?
- Where did I learn that exploration should be "proper"?
- How is my need for order affecting my child's discovery?

Type Five Parents like Priya might unconsciously limit exploration to manage energy:

- Restricting intense engagement
- Preferring observation over interaction
- Missing opportunities for physical discovery

But curiosity about their pattern can transform this:

- Why am I so uncomfortable with energetic exploration?
- What happens in my body when things get too intense?
- How might my withdrawal limit my child's growth?

The Patterning Years (3-6): Questions and Connections

As children enter the patterning years, curiosity takes on new dimensions. Physical exploration continues but is joined by increasingly sophisticated cognitive and social investigation. Watch five-year-old Marcus's endless "why" questions. They're not just about gathering information but about understanding how the world works and how he fits within it.

This period brings:

- Complex question sequences
- Imaginative hypothesis testing
- Social experimentation
- Pattern recognition and creation

Watch four-year-old Lucas building with blocks. When his tower falls, multiple opportunities arise:

- For his natural curiosity: Why did it fall? What if I try it differently?
- For Rachel's (3) pattern: Let me show you the right way
- For Rachel's potential growth: What makes me so quick to fix things?

This is where conscious work with curiosity becomes crucial. When parents learn to get curious about their patterns, they create space for their children's natural exploration to flourish. They can join their child in genuine discovery instead of rushing to fix, show, or manage.

Common Scenarios Where Patterns Meet Curiosity

Consider these everyday moments where parent patterns interact with children's natural exploration:

Emma at Art Time

Natural Curiosity:

- Experimenting with color mixing
- Testing different brush strokes
- Discovering new techniques

Sarah's (1) pattern response:

- Demonstrating "correct" methods
- Managing mess anxiety

- Guiding toward "better" results

But when transformed by curiosity:

- Noticing perfectionist impulse
- Wondering about control needs
- Staying present with exploration

Maya in Nature

Natural Curiosity:

- Collecting unusual rocks
- Following ant trails
- Making mud experiments

Priya's (5) pattern response:

- Providing information
- Managing energy drain
- Maintaining distance

When transformed by curiosity:

- Noticing withdrawal impulse
- Exploring energy management
- Staying engaged while respecting needs

Understanding these developmental stages and how they interact with our patterns gives us unprecedented opportunities to support our children's natural curiosity and our growth. The goal isn't to maintain childlike wonder forever but to help ensure that curiosity can continue serving development throughout life.

Working with Patterns through Curiosity

Observe this scene: Five-year-old Emma is deeply absorbed in painting, mixing colors freely, her art materials spread across the table. Sarah (1) feels the familiar tension rising—the urge to contain the mess, direct the activity, and maintain order. But instead of immediately stepping in to manage, she pauses and gets curious about her reaction.

"What's happening in my body right now?" she wonders. She notices the tightness in her chest and the slight acceleration of breath. "Where did I learn that creativity should be neat?" The simple act of wondering starts to create space around her pattern. As she stays curious about her reaction, she can watch Emma's natural exploration with less need to control.

Head Center Patterns

Type Five Parents (Priya)

Watch how curiosity transforms her interaction with Maya.

- Noticing the urge to withdraw
- Getting curious about her need for distance
- Wondering about her own childhood experiences
- Exploring her relationship with engagement

Through this curiosity, she finds ways to move slightly closer while still honoring personal comfort. Instead of automatically stepping back when Maya's exploration becomes intense, she stays present with her discomfort, discovering new possibilities for engagement.

Type Six Parents (Michael)

Emma's father feels his anxiety spike when she climbs higher on the jungle gym. Instead of calling out, "Be careful!" he gets curious.

- What am I afraid of here?
- How much of this fear is from my past?
- What does Emma's body language tell me about her capability?
- How might my anxiety limit her growth?

Type Seven Parents (Raj)

Maya's father notices his tendency to redirect her away from complicated feelings. His pattern wants to keep things light and fun. Getting curious helps.

- Why am I uncomfortable with her frustration?
- What happens to me when things slow down?
- Where did I learn that everything should be upbeat?
- How might my avoidance affect her development?

Heart Center Patterns

Type Two Parents (Ana)

Sofia's mother watches her struggle with a puzzle, feeling the urge to help. Her curiosity reveals:

- What makes it so hard to watch her struggle?
- Why do I feel I need to help to be valuable?
- What happens in my body when I resist helping?
- How might my help affect her independence?

Type Three Parents (Rachel)

Lucas's mother feels her pattern activate when he shows no interest in "educational activities." Curiosity helps.

- Why am I so invested in his performance?
- What am I afraid might happen if we just play?
- Where did I learn that everything must be productive?
- How might my achievement-focus shape his self-worth?

Type Four Parents (Carlos)

Sofia's father notices his desire to make an ordinary moment extraordinary. His curiosity reveals:

- Why do I need this experience to be special?
- What happens in me when things feel mundane?
- Where did I learn that ordinary moments aren't enough?
- How might my intensity affect her simple enjoyment?

Body Center Patterns

Type Eight Parents (Lisa)

Watch Marcus's mother with her son. Her curiosity reveals:

- What makes me need to take charge?
- Where did I learn that control equals safety?
- What happens when I let my child lead?
- How might my strength affect his vulnerability?

Type Nine Parents (David)

Marcus's father notices his tendency to go along with whatever his son wants. His curiosity helps.

- Why is it so hard for me to assert my preferences?
- What am I afraid might happen if I disagree?
- Where did I learn that peace matters more than my needs?
- How might my accommodating affect his understanding of boundaries?

Type One Parents (Sarah)

Emma's mother feels her pattern activate when art time gets messy. Curiosity reveals:

- Why does disorder create such tension in me?
- What am I afraid might happen if things aren't neat?
- Where did I learn that "right" means orderly?

- How might my perfectionism affect her creative expression?

Daily Life with Curiosity

Everyday moments offer rich opportunities for working with our patterns and our children's development. Consider these typical scenarios.

Morning Rush

Watch this familiar scene: It's 8:15 AM, Maya and Priya (5) are running late, and Maya has just discovered a fascinating beetle on the front step. Priya's pattern activates immediately, pushing for energy conservation, time management, and controlled engagement. But this moment holds an opportunity for both of them.

Instead of reacting from the pattern:

- Pause and notice your automatic response
- Get curious about your reaction: What's happening in me right now?
- Wonder about your child's experience: What are they discovering?
- Allow space for both need sets: How can we honor time and wonder?

Through curiosity, rigid patterns soften, allowing for growth, connection, and a more open approach to parenting. Each challenging moment becomes an opportunity to examine our patterns while supporting our children's natural development.

The Path Forward

When parents learn to work with their patterns through curiosity, they transform their lives and their children's developmental environment. Instead of unconsciously passing on rigid patterns:

- Type One parents move from controlling to wondering
- Type Two parents shift from managing to witnessing
- Type Three parents transform from achieving to being
- Type Four parents flow from dramatizing to experiencing
- Type Five parents evolve from distancing to engaging

- Type Six parents grow from worrying to exploring
- Type Seven parents deepen from avoiding to staying present
- Type Eight parents soften from directing to supporting
- Type Nine parents awaken from merging to participating

Through this conscious engagement:

- Rigid patterns become flexible responses
- Protective strategies maintain their wisdom
- Natural development flourishes
- Authentic connection deepens

The Sacred Dance

Your child's curiosity isn't just something to protect. It's an invitation to rediscover your capacity for wonder. Each challenging moment offers an opportunity for mutual growth and deeper connection.

The journey isn't about perfection but presence:

- Staying curious about your reactions
- Wondering about your patterns
- Maintaining space for growth
- Supporting natural development

This is the sacred dance of early childhood. We do not prevent patterns from forming but support their development with enough flexibility that they can continue growing and adapting throughout life. Through conscious engagement with our patterns and support for our children's natural curiosity, we create the conditions for genuine growth and development at every age.

Transitioning from our exploration of curiosity to examining the sacred art of seeing, reflect on how your Type's approach to wonder influences your capacity for truly recognizing your child. Your relationship with not-knowing—through engagement, analysis, or reframing—shapes how you create an environment where your child feels genuinely seen. In the next chapter, we'll discover how your Type's characteristic patterns around recognition create the atmosphere in which your child develops their sense of being valued. We'll see how your approach to seeing influences your child's emerging sense of their worth and visibility.

Reflection

Take a few quiet moments to explore your relationship with curiosity—your natural wonder and your learned patterns around exploration. Notice how your Type's particular focus influences your comfort with the unknown.

Your Pattern's Dance with Wonder

Consider your automatic responses to exploration.

- What aspects of discovery activate your pattern?
- How does your Type typically manage uncertainty?
- Where do you feel most challenged by your child's curiosity?
- What helps you stay present with not knowing?

Living Laboratory

Think about a recent moment of discovery with your child.

- What happened in your body?
- How did your pattern want to respond?
- Where did you find flexibility?
- What supported your ability to stay present?

Remember: Curiosity is the antidote to fixed patterns. When we genuinely wonder about ourselves, our patterns, and our children's unique way of being, we create space for authentic growth and connection.

Your Notes

Chapter 9

The Sacred Art of Seeing

To be seen is to be known, and to be known is to belong.
Martin Buber

As we explore the art of genuinely seeing our children, we'll discover how different personality patterns influence our capacity for presence and recognition. We'll see how early experiences with being seen shape development and how conscious awareness can transform both parent and child.

Five-year-old Sofia has just finished telling an elaborate story about her day at school. Her mother Ana (2) feels her pattern activate—the urge to praise, to show how closely she's been listening, to ensure Sofia feels deeply seen. Her father Carlos (4) experiences his response—the impulse to amplify the emotional significance of the moment, to make it special. This simple interaction shows how different Types' patterns influence their capacity for genuine presence.

Watch what happens next. Ana catches her helping pattern and pauses before jumping in with praise. She notices her body's familiar tension: the need to demonstrate attention, to prove her worth through careful listening. Carlos feels his intensifying impulse, the desire to make this ordinary moment extraordinary. But today, something different occurs. Instead of acting from these patterns, they sit with Sofia in the glow of her storytelling, their presence arising not from strategy but from genuine connection.

The longing to be truly seen reflects our soul's desire for recognition. When we say "I see you" deeply, we acknowledge the eternal, unchanging essence that exists before and beyond all personality patterns. Each Type brings its particular challenges and gifts to this sacred act of seeing.

Type One parents like Sarah struggle with seeing beyond their ideals and standards, their pattern urging them to notice what needs improvement rather than what simply is.

Type Two parents like Ana face the challenge of seeing without needing to demonstrate their attention, their pattern pulling them to prove their presence through active response.

Type Three parents like Rachel must work with their tendency to see through the lens of performance and achievement, their pattern focused on doing rather than being.

Type Four parents like Carlos encounter the challenge of seeing the ordinary without needing to make it special. Their pattern is drawn to intensify experiences rather than accept them as they are.

Type Five parents like Priya contend with seeing directly rather than through analysis, their pattern inclined to understand rather than witness what is present.

Type Six parents like Michael work with seeing clearly without scanning for problems. Their pattern is oriented toward anticipating difficulties rather than trusting the present moment.

Type Seven parents like Raj face the challenge of seeing what is rather than what could be, their pattern drawn to possibilities rather than present reality.

Type Eight parents like Lisa must work with seeing vulnerability without controlling it, their pattern focused on strength and protection rather than accepting gentleness.

Type Nine parents like David encounter the challenge of seeing distinctly rather than merging, their pattern inclined toward harmony and agreement rather than recognizing differences.

Understanding how our patterns influence our capacity for presence gives us unprecedented opportunities to develop deeper recognition of our children's authentic nature. Our role isn't to achieve perfect seeing—that's neither possible nor necessary—but to become increasingly conscious of how our patterns filter our perception while developing greater flexibility in our ways of being present.

The Three Practices of Seeing

Genuine recognition requires three distinct yet interrelated practices: acknowledgment, mirroring, and praise. Each Type brings particular challenges and gifts to these practices, influencing how children experience being seen.

1. Acknowledgment

Watch how different parents navigate simple acknowledgment.

Sarah (1) observes Emma drawing.

Without awareness, she might:

- Focus on technique and improvement
- Notice what needs correction
- Miss the joy of pure expression
- Filter through standards

Through conscious work, she learns to:

- See without judging
- Notice without correcting
- Witness without improving
- Acknowledge what is

Rachel (3) watches Lucas perform.

Without awareness, she might:

- Focus on achievement aspects
- Notice performance elements
- Miss the simple pleasure
- Filter through success metrics

Through development, she learns to:

- See beyond accomplishment
- Notice authentic expression
- Witness without evaluation
- Acknowledge pure being

2. Mirroring

Priya (5) observes Maya exploring.

Without awareness, she might:

- Analyze rather than reflect
- Create distance through observation
- Miss emotional resonance
- Filter through understanding

Through conscious work, she learns to:

- Mirror without interpretation
- Stay present with experience
- Reflect emotional truth
- Acknowledge direct knowing

Lisa (8) watches Marcus assert himself.

Without awareness, she might:

- Amplify power aspects
- Miss subtle vulnerabilities
- Over-mirror strength
- Filter through protection

Through development, she learns to:

- Mirror balanced strength
- Reflect full experience
- Honor all expressions
- Acknowledge gentle power

3. Praise

Ana (2) responds to Sofia's achievements.

Without awareness, she might:

- Over-praise to ensure feeling seen
- Make each moment significant
- Miss simple recognition
- Filter through helping

Through conscious work, she learns to:

- Praise with authenticity
- Recognize without amplifying
- Celebrate naturally
- Acknowledge genuinely

Carlos (4) witnesses Sofia's uniqueness.

Without awareness, he might:

- Intensify special qualities
- Make ordinary moments dramatic
- Miss simple presence
- Filter through significance

Through development, he learns to:

- Celebrate without dramatizing
- Recognize natural uniqueness
- Honor ordinary moments
- Acknowledge authentic being

How might you offer appropriate and genuine praise to support your child?

The Integration of Seeing

True seeing emerges when these three practices work together.

- Acknowledgment provides the ground of acceptance
- Mirroring offers accurate reflection
- Praise celebrates authentic expression

Watch this integration in action:

Emma shows Sarah (1) her painting:

- Acknowledgment sees without judgment
- Mirroring reflects her engagement
- Praise celebrates her natural expression

Through conscious work with their patterns, parents develop the capacity to see their children beyond their Type's particular filters. This doesn't mean abandoning their

- Use enthusiasm to appreciate what is
- Find joy in the immediate moment
- Turn planning into attentive witnessing

Daily life reveals this transformation when Maya shares a difficult feeling. Instead of quickly reframing or moving to the next activity, Raj practices staying with the current experience, allowing Maya's full emotional range to be seen and acknowledged.

Heart Center Patterns

Common Challenges:

- Seeking identity through others' responses
- Shaping self to match others' expectations
- Finding worth through emotional impact

Type Two Parents (Ana)

Watch Ana's pattern influence her way of seeing Sofia.

Without awareness, she might:

- Over-demonstrate attention
- Make each moment significant
- Miss simple presence
- Filter through helping

Through conscious work, she learns to:

- Transform helping into presence
- Use attunement for genuine connection
- Find worth through being rather than doing
- Turn care into recognition

Sofia's daily life shows this transformation when she shares her experiences. Ana practices simple witnessing instead of jumping to respond or help, allowing Sofia's experience to unfold naturally.

Type Three Parents (Rachel)

Observe how Rachel's pattern shapes her recognition of Lucas.

Without awareness, she might:

- Focus on performance aspects
- Miss simple being
- Filter through achievement
- Seek worth through success

Through development, she learns to:

- Transform doing into presence
- Use accomplishment to celebrate being
- Find value beyond achievement
- Turn success into appreciation

Type Four Parents (Carlos)

Watch how Carlos's pattern influences his way of seeing Sofia.

Without awareness, he might:

- Search for what's unique or special
- Miss ordinary moments of connection
- Filter through emotional significance
- Seek depth in every interaction

Through conscious work, he learns to:

- Transform intensity into presence

- Use sensitivity to appreciate simplicity
- Find meaning in everyday experiences
- Turn emotional depth into quiet recognition

Daily interactions reveal this transformation when Sofia shares a simple joy. Instead of amplifying or making the moment more significant, Carlos practices being present with its ordinariness, allowing Sofia's genuine experience to exist without embellishment.

Body Center Patterns

Common Challenges:

- Equating strength with value
- Merging to maintain connection
- Seeking worth through correctness

Type Eight Parents (Lisa)

Watch how Lisa's pattern influences her way of seeing Marcus.

Without awareness, she might:

- Focus on power dynamics
- Miss subtle expressions
- Filter through strength
- Seek control in recognition

Through conscious work, she learns to:

- Transform protection into presence
- Use strength to hold space
- Find security through vulnerability
- Turn power into appreciation

When Marcus explores his world, his daily interactions show this transformation. Instead of immediately stepping in to protect or direct, Lisa practices holding space with strength that doesn't overwhelm.

Type Nine Parents (David)

Notice how David's pattern shapes his recognition of Marcus.

Without awareness, he might:

- Merge with the child's experience
- Miss distinct individuality
- Filter through harmony
- Seek comfort in recognition

Through development, he learns to:

- Transform merging into presence
- Use peacefulness to create space
- Find connection while maintaining boundaries
- Turn accommodation into clear seeing

Daily life reveals this transformation when Marcus expresses a preference different from David's. Instead of automatically accommodating or withdrawing, David practices staying present with the difference, allowing Marcus's distinct self to be truly seen.

Type One Parents (Sarah)

Notice how Sarah's pattern shapes her recognition of Emma.

Without awareness, she might:

- Look for what needs improvement
- Miss natural perfection
- Filter through standards
- Seek correctness in recognition

Through development, she learns to:

- Transform correction into presence
- Use discernment to deepen seeing
- Find rightness in what is
- Turn improvement into appreciation

The goal isn't to eliminate these patterns but to develop enough flexibility that they can serve rather than limit our capacity for seeing. Through conscious work with our patterns, we create space for more authentic recognition of our children's being.

Human Qualities to Acknowledge

Certain fundamental qualities deserve special recognition in our practice of seeing children. Not because praising them will create them—these qualities are inherent in every child—but because acknowledging them helps children recognize and value these aspects of themselves.

Nine qualities worthy of acknowledgment:

Courage	Recognizing when children face challenges helps them trust their inner resources.
Curiosity	Celebrating a child's natural wonder and questioning supports their innate drive to learn and explore.
Effort	Recognizing a child's dedication and persistence, regardless of outcome, validates their internal motivation and builds resilience.
Empathy	Noting when children recognize and respond to others' feelings reinforces their inherent capacity for emotional connection.
Honesty	Recognizing truthfulness, especially when difficult, supports the development of integrity.
Independence	Celebrating their steps toward autonomy validates their growing sense of capability.
Kindness	Acknowledging moments of compassion and consideration helps children value their natural capacity for caring.
Patience	Acknowledging their capacity to wait and persist supports emotional regulation development.

Resilience	Acknowledging their ability to recover and adapt helps children trust their inner strength.

These qualities aren't behaviors to be shaped but natural capacities to be recognized and supported. When we acknowledge them, we help children discover these strengths within themselves rather than trying to develop them from outside.

Integration and Moving Forward

Remember that each moment offers an opportunity to reinforce patterns or create space for authentic being. Through conscious acknowledgment, accurate mirroring, and being-centered praise, we help our children feel genuinely seen in their essence, not for what they do, achieve, or present, but for who they fundamentally are.

This is the profound gift of conscious parenting: learning to see our children beyond our patterns, beyond their behaviors, and even beyond their emerging personality structures, to witness and celebrate the sacred mystery of their being as it unfolds before us.

In this practice of true seeing, both parent and child are transformed. We discover that acknowledgment, mirroring, and praise aren't techniques to master but invitations to presence, opportunities to meet our children in the sacred territory where being meets being, where patterns soften into possibility, and where love reveals itself as the simple art of seeing and being seen.

As we shift from examining the sacred art of seeing to exploring the sacred dance of development, consider how your Type's approach to recognition influences your capacity for the ongoing dance of parenting. Your particular way of seeing—filtered through your Type's lens—shapes how you create an environment of mutual discovery with your child. In the final chapter, we'll combine all we've explored to understand how your Type's patterns can maintain enough flexibility to support your child's authentic development. We'll see how conscious engagement with your patterns creates the foundation for your growth and your child's lifelong resilience.

Reflection

Take a few quiet moments to explore how you see your child, noticing the filters your Type brings to recognition.

Your Pattern of Seeing

Notice how your Type influences the way you look.

- What aspects of your child do you naturally focus on?
- What tends to fall into your blind spots?
- How does your pattern filter what you see?
- Where do you find yourself looking through expectations rather than seeing what is?

Creating Space for True Seeing

Consider what supports your capacity to see clearly.

- What helps you slow down enough to really look?
- How do you catch yourself when projection arises?
- What allows you to set aside your Type's usual filters?
- What supports your ability to stay present with what is?

Remember: True seeing is a gift that transforms both the seer and the seen. When we learn to look beyond our patterns and projections, we create space for our children's authentic nature to flourish.

Your Notes

Chapter 10

The Sacred Dance of Development

The most precious gift we can offer others is our presence. When mindfulness embraces those we love, they will bloom like flowers.

Thich Nhat Hanh

As we conclude our exploration, we discover how all the elements we've examined—acceptance, attachment, anger, fear, shame, the superego, curiosity, and seeing—come together in the sacred dance of development. This dance requires structure, flexibility, pattern, and possibility.

Watch this moment unfold: Six-year-old Emma stands before her latest artwork, her whole body radiating uncertainty. Her mother Sarah (1) feels her familiar pattern arise—the urge to assess, guide, and improve. But today, drawing on all we've explored, she pauses. In this space between pattern and presence, she feels:

- Her Type One perfectionism activating
- The inherited voices of her superego
- Her child's need for true acceptance
- The opportunity for genuine seeing

Instead of responding from her pattern, she stays with the moment, allowing Emma's experience and her own to exist without needing to change. This is the sacred dance—the ability to hold pattern and possibility, structure and freedom.

Throughout our journey, we've witnessed how personality patterns emerge through:

- The fundamental need for acceptance

- The web of early attachment
- The expression of vital anger
- The protection of fear
- The shaping force of shame
- The consolidation of the superego
- The flame of curiosity
- The art of true seeing

Now we discover how these elements work together to support healthy development while maintaining flexibility for continued growth. This isn't about achieving perfect parenting—that's neither possible nor desirable—but about developing enough awareness to dance with our patterns rather than being confined by them.

Each Type brings particular gifts and challenges to this dance:

Type One parents like Sarah must balance:

- Structure with flexibility
- Standards with acceptance
- Improvement with appreciation
- Guidance with freedom

Type Two parents like Ana navigate:

- Helping with allowing
- Connection with independence
- Care with space
- Attunement with autonomy

Type Three parents like Rachel balance:

- Achievement with presence
- Performance with authenticity

- Success with process
- Goals with exploration

Type Four parents like Carlos navigate:

- Depth with simplicity
- Uniqueness with ordinariness
- Intensity with calm
- Significance with acceptance

Type Five parents like Priya balance:

- Knowledge with experience
- Observation with engagement
- Analysis with presence
- Independence with connection

Type Six parents like Michael navigate:

- Caution with trust
- Vigilance with openness
- Planning with spontaneity
- Security with adventure

Type Seven parents like Raj balance:

- Possibilities with presence
- Excitement with depth
- Options with commitment
- Stimulation with stillness

Type Eight parents like Lisa navigate:

- Protection with vulnerability

- Strength with gentleness
- Control with allowing
- Directness with receptivity

Type Nine parents like David balance:

- Peace with engagement
- Harmony with differentiation
- Accommodation with assertion
- Comfort with challenge

Understanding how these patterns participate in the dance of development gives us unprecedented opportunities to support our children's growth and our own evolution. Our role isn't to lead perfectly but to stay present in the dance, responsive to the moment's unique demands while maintaining awareness of our patterns' influence.

Three Essential Understandings

1. The Living Laboratory of Pattern Formation

Every interaction between parent and child becomes part of the living laboratory where personality patterns take shape. Watch these moments unfold.

- Maya's quiet withdrawal meeting Priya's (5) tendency toward distance
- Marcus's strong assertion encountering Lisa's (8) comfort with power
- Sofia's emotional intensity activating Ana's (2) helping pattern
- Lucas's achievement focus reflecting Rachel's (3) success orientation

These aren't just isolated moments but the threads from which personality patterns are woven. Understanding this active process gives us unprecedented opportunities to support healthy development while maintaining maximum flexibility in pattern formation.

2. The Parent's Journey as Primary Ground

Perhaps our most crucial discovery has been that the parent's personal growth work creates the foundation for everything else. No amount of positive parenting techniques or behavioral strategies can prevent the transmission of rigid patterns if parents haven't done their deep work. Watch how this truth reveals itself.

- Sarah's (1) work with perfectionism creates space for Emma's natural expression
- Priya's (5) examination of withdrawal allows Maya's authentic engagement
- Lisa's (8) exploration of protection supports Marcus's gentle strength
- Ana's (2) investigation of helping enables Sofia's genuine independence

This understanding transforms how we approach supporting children's development. Instead of focusing solely on techniques or strategies, we recognize that our growth work becomes the ground from which genuine presence can emerge.

3. The Dance of Flexibility and Structure

We aim not to prevent patterns from forming; that's neither possible nor desirable. Instead, we work to support their development with enough flexibility so they can continue growing and adapting throughout life. This delicate balance reveals itself in daily moments.

- Emma learning that mistakes can be both informative and acceptable
- Maya discovering she can maintain boundaries while staying connected
- Marcus experiencing that strength can coexist with tenderness
- Sofia finding that emotions can be both intense and contained

Through conscious engagement with our patterns, we create conditions for genuine growth and resilience while supporting our children's natural development.

The Integration in Daily Life

Watch how these understandings transform everyday moments.

Sarah (1) with Emma:

- Noticing perfectionist impulses arise
- Feeling the inherited critic activate
- Choosing presence over pattern
- Creating space for authentic expression

Ana (2) with Sofia:

- Recognizing helping impulses surface
- Feeling the urge to manage emotions
- Choosing witnessing over fixing
- Creating space for independent growth

Rachel (3) with Lucas:

- Noticing achievement focus emerge
- Feeling the drive for performance
- Choosing being over doing
- Creating space for process over outcome

Carlos (4) with Sofia:

- Recognizing intensifying tendencies
- Feeling the pull toward significance
- Choosing simplicity over drama
- Creating space for ordinary joy

Priya (5) with Maya:

- Recognizing withdrawal tendencies
- Experiencing knowledge seeking urges
- Staying present with intensity

- Supporting natural exploration

Michael (6) with Emma:

- Noticing vigilant scanning activate
- Feeling anxiety about potential problems
- Choosing trust over worry
- Creating space for healthy risk-taking

Raj (7) with Maya:

- Recognizing planning impulses arise
- Feeling the urge to move to the next thing
- Choosing presence with difficulty
- Creating space for depth and completion

Lisa (8) with Marcus:

- Noticing protective instincts surface
- Feeling the drive to take control
- Choosing containment over dominance
- Creating space for gentle strength

David (9) with Marcus:

- Recognizing merging tendencies
- Feeling the pull toward accommodation
- Choosing clear boundaries while staying connected
- Creating space for healthy differentiation

These moments of integration aren't about achieving perfection but about maintaining enough awareness to work consciously with our patterns while supporting our children's development. Through this understanding, we create environments where structure and flexibility can serve growth.

Each Type brings unique gifts to this integration:

- **Type One** parents offer healthy structure
- **Type Two** parents provide emotional attunement
- **Type Three** parents support achievement
- **Type Four** parents honor uniqueness
- **Type Five** parents value understanding
- **Type Six** parents ensure safety
- **Type Seven** parents encourage possibilities
- **Type Eight** parents protect growth
- **Type Nine** parents maintain peace

The sacred dance emerges when we can hold our pattern's wisdom and the space for something new to emerge.

The Path Forward

Every step on this journey offers opportunities for growth through deepening self-understanding and conscious presence with our children. Watch how different families integrate these understandings.

The Connor Family Practice (Types 1 and 6)

Sarah (1) and Michael (6) work with their patterns by:

- Balancing structure with flexibility
- Supporting natural development
- Maintaining loving presence
- Creating space for authenticity

Through conscious engagement, they learn to:

- Notice perfectionist and anxious impulses
- Stay present with uncertainty

- Allow natural unfolding
- Trust the development process

The Patel Family Integration (Types 5 and 7)

Priya (5) and Raj (7) develop their approach by:

- Balancing distance with connection
- Supporting gradual engagement
- Maintaining steady presence
- Creating space for exploration

Their growth involves:

- Noticing withdrawal and avoidance patterns
- Staying engaged with challenge
- Allowing natural rhythm
- Trusting emotional process

The Chen Family Practice (Types 8 and 9)

Lisa (8) and David (9) work with their patterns by:

- Balancing protection with peace
- Supporting strength with gentleness
- Maintaining clear boundaries
- Creating space for both assertion and harmony

Through conscious engagement, they learn to:

- Notice controlling and merging impulses
- Stay present with differences
- Allow natural leadership to emerge
- Trust the balance of power and connection

The Rodriguez Family Integration (Types 2 and 4)

Ana (2) and Carlos (4) develop their approach by:

- Balancing helping with depth
- Supporting emotional expression
- Maintaining authentic connection
- Creating space for both ordinary and special moments

Their growth involves:

- Noticing rescuing and intensifying patterns
- Staying present with emotional complexity
- Allowing independence alongside connection
- Trusting their child's emotional journey

The Smith Family Practice (Types 1 and 3)

Rachel (3) and James (1) work with their patterns by:

- Balancing achievement with acceptance
- Supporting excellence without perfectionism
- Maintaining presence beyond performance
- Creating space for both success and process

Through conscious engagement, they learn to:

- Notice image-focused and critical impulses
- Stay present with imperfection
- Allow natural development beyond goals
- Trust growth beyond measurable outcomes

The Sacred Art of Being Present

The ultimate gift we offer our children isn't perfect parenting but conscious presence. This means:

- Recognizing our patterns without being bound by them
- Supporting development without controlling it
- Maintaining connection through difficulty
- Creating space for authentic being

Through understanding how personality patterns form while maintaining flexibility in development, we help create the conditions for:

- Healthier personality development
- More flexible response patterns
- Greater emotional resilience
- Deeper authentic connection

This sacred dance transforms both parent and child, creating spaces where:

- Patterns can serve rather than constrain
- Growth can unfold naturally
- Connection can deepen authentically
- Being can flourish freely

Reflection

Take a few quiet moments to consider your sacred dance of development with your child, both the patterns that structure your interaction and the spaces where new possibilities emerge.

Your Dance of Development

Notice how your Type influences your movement.

- What aspects of development activate your pattern?
- Where do you find natural rhythm with your child?
- How does your pattern support structure?
- What helps you maintain flexibility?

The Living Partnership

Consider a recent moment of connection.

- What patterns arose in you?
- How did you work with them?
- Where did you find freedom?
- What supported your presence?

Remember: The sacred dance isn't about achieving perfection but about maintaining enough awareness to work consciously with our patterns while supporting our children's natural development.

Your Notes

Thank You for Sharing This Journey

Thank you for engaging in this deep exploration of Enneagram personality patterns and parenting. Your willingness to examine your own Type's influence while maintaining presence with your child's authentic development is sacred work that ripples through generations.

Remember that this conscious parenting journey unfolds gradually, one moment of awareness at a time. Each time you catch your pattern and choose presence over automatic reaction, you create space for your child and you to develop more flexibly and authentically.

For additional resources, exercises, and support in your continuing journey, please visit:

EnneagramWorldOfTheChild.com

To connect directly with the author or share your experience:

EnneaChild@gmail.com

Through your grace, the world heals,

John Harper

Afterward

Throughout this book, we've explored how personality patterns emerge through the dance between child and parent, between nature and nurture, and between inherited tendencies and environmental influences. At the heart of our exploration lies a profound truth: The extraordinary plasticity of the developing brain offers unprecedented opportunities for nurturing resilience and flexibility in our children.

When we understand that a child's brain contains approximately 100 billion neurons at birth and forms trillions of connections in response to early experiences, we grasp the profound responsibility and extraordinary opportunity before us. Every interaction—from Emma's careful artwork to Maya's quiet observation, from Marcus's bold explorations to Sofia's emotional expressions—shapes not just momentary behavior but the very architecture of the developing brain.

The neuroscience principle—"what fires, gets wired"—illuminates how these daily interactions create the neural foundations of personality. Each time Sarah (1) responds to Emma's perfectionist struggles with presence rather than correction, those neurons fire together, strengthening pathways of self-acceptance. When Priya (5) maintains connection while honoring Maya's need for space, she helps wire circuits that balance autonomy with relationship. As Lisa (8) finds ways to contain Marcus's intensity while celebrating his strength, she supports the development of neural networks that integrate power with wisdom.

This understanding makes it crucial for Enneagram-informed parents to "hang loose" with typing their children. When we understand how the primary emotional forces—anger, fear, and shame—shape early development, we see why premature typing can interfere with our children's natural unfolding. While the temptation to type our children is understandable, when we relate to them through the lens of a specific Type, we risk relating to our idea of who they are rather than the mystery of their actual being. We unconsciously pressure them to conform to our understanding rather than allowing their authentic nature to emerge.

Our exploration shows that humans are far more dynamic and fluid than any pattern suggests. The Enneagram's emotional triads illuminate three ways of coping with each primary emotion: overemphasis, neutralization, and suppression. Like a prism splitting light into its component colors, each triad reveals different adaptations to the same fundamental emotional force.

Consider how this plays out with anger, the vital life force that helps children define themselves and assert their boundaries. The Type Eight pattern overemphasizes anger, amplifying its force to feel powerful and protected. The Type Nine pattern neutralizes anger, muting its expression to maintain peace and connection. The Type One pattern suppresses anger, channeling it into self-control and improvement. Yet any parent of a young child knows that the same child who fiercely defends their toy one moment might seek peaceful compromise the next or channel their frustration into careful organization later that day.

Similar dynamics emerge with fear in the Head Center. The Type Six pattern demonstrates two distinct responses to fear, either moving toward it through vigilance and preparation (phobic) or moving against it through direct confrontation and courage (counterphobic). The Type Five pattern neutralizes fear through understanding and distance, while the Type Seven pattern suppresses fear by moving toward positive possibilities. Watch Maya at the playground: in one moment, she might carefully assess a new climbing structure like a Type Five, then seek reassurance from some children while boldly challenging others like a Type Six before enthusiastically exploring multiple activities like a Type Seven.

With shame in the Heart Center, we see the Type Four pattern overemphasizing shame by intensifying emotional depth to maintain uniqueness, the Type Three pattern neutralizing shame through achievement and image, and the Type Two pattern suppressing shame by focusing on others' needs. Sofia might express Type Four-like sensitivity during art time, shift to Type Three-like performance in dance class, and display Type Two-like helping with younger children—all authentic expressions of her developing self.

While we may have a primary fixation or habitual way of coping, we are, in fact, all nine Types. The Enneagram's intricate system of wings and lines of connection reflects this fundamental truth: We contain all these possibilities, expressing different aspects as circumstances and development require. This dynamic nature is particularly evident in how we manage primary emotions. In one moment, a parent might overemphasize anger to protect their child from danger, in another, neutralize it to maintain family harmony, and, in yet another, suppress it to model self-control.

Understanding this natural dynamism transforms how we support our children's development. Instead of trying to identify or shape a fixed pattern, we celebrate the full range of their emotional expressions, support their exploration of different coping strategies, and help them develop flexibility in responding to life's challenges. We trust their innate wisdom in finding what works in various situations.

This understanding aligns perfectly with what neuroscience tells us about brain plasticity. Just as neural pathways strengthen through repeated use but maintain the potential for new connections, our personality patterns can be both stable enough to provide coherence and flexible enough to allow growth. When we understand how repeated experiences wire neural circuits together, we see why early childhood offers profound opportunities for supporting healthy development.

Consider the patterns we've explored throughout the book. Emma's careful erasing becomes rigid perfectionism or healthy striving, depending on how her parents respond to her struggles. Maya's thoughtful observation develops into fearful withdrawal or wise discernment, shaped by how her environment honors her natural rhythm. Marcus's strong assertions transform into either defensive aggression or confident strength, influenced by how his parents contain and support his energy.

Each interaction fires neurons together, creating and strengthening pathways that become the foundation of personality. When we respond to our children with conscious presence rather than reactive patterns, we help wire their brains for flexibility rather than rigidity, resilience rather than fragility, curiosity rather than certainty, and connection rather than isolation.

This understanding transforms our approach to challenging moments. When Lucas struggles with performance anxiety or Sofia faces social uncertainty, we recognize these aren't just behavioral issues to manage but opportunities to help wire their brains for greater adaptability and resilience. The brain's remarkable plasticity during early childhood means that every time we pause before reacting, get curious about our patterns, maintain presence through difficulty, support rather than suppress, and accept rather than judge, we're helping establish neural pathways that will serve our children throughout their lives.

Our goal isn't to prevent patterns from forming; that's neither possible nor desirable. Instead, we want to support healthy development while maintaining enough flexibility so these patterns can continue growing and adapting throughout life. This requires us to relate to our children as emerging mysteries rather than fixed Types, bringing curiosity and presence to each interaction rather than categorical understanding.

By consciously engaging with our patterns while supporting our children's natural development, we create conditions for genuine growth and resilience at every age. Each challenging moment allows both parent and child to develop greater flexibility and deeper connection. When we understand the profound plasticity of the developing brain and honor the dynamic nature of personality development, we can create environments that support our children's natural unfolding while maintaining the flexibility needed for lifelong growth and adaptation.

This is the sacred work of parenting: not preventing patterns from forming but supporting their development with enough flexibility that they can continue growing and adapting throughout life. As we learn to hold our children's emerging selves with curiosity and wonder, we create a container of love that allows their unique essence to flourish. And in that space of witnessing, we too are changed, growing into more spacious and authentic versions of ourselves.

The Enneagram World of the Child reveals itself as more than individual personality development; it is the dynamic interplay between the family ecosystem, shaped by the parents' patterns, and the child's emerging emotional subjectivity. Perhaps this book's most profound insight is that supporting our children's healthy development begins with us, the parents.

Our children don't need fixing or shaping; they need us to loosen our fixated patterns, develop greater flexibility in our responses, and expand our capacity for presence. Examining and loosening our personality patterns creates a more spacious and adaptable family ecosystem where our children can naturally thrive. As we develop more remarkable plasticity in our responses, more resilience in our emotional capacity, and increased flexibility in our ways of being, we offer our children the most incredible gift possible. This environment supports their authentic unfolding while maintaining the freedom to grow and adapt.

This is the sacred opportunity of conscious parenting: not to shape our children into what we think they should be but to transform ourselves so we and they can discover who they truly are.

Appendix. Parenting Patterns of the Nine Types

The Enneagram is a model that describes nine distinct personality Types and their complex interrelationships, with each Type having its core motivations, fears, and behavior patterns. Each person has a dominant Type (numbered 1-9) that shapes their fundamental way of seeing and interacting with the world. However, they may also display traits of other Types, particularly under stress or during personal growth. The system suggests that while we're born with certain tendencies, understanding our Type can help us recognize our patterns and develop greater self-awareness and emotional intelligence.

Note: *These patterns describe tendencies that parents of each Type may experience. Each parent is unique and may express these patterns differently based on their individual development, life experiences, and level of self-awareness. Understanding these patterns can help parents become more conscious of their natural tendencies and better support their children's authentic development.*

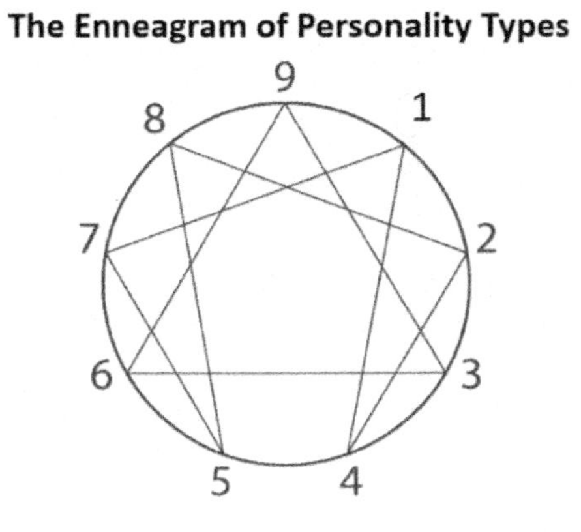

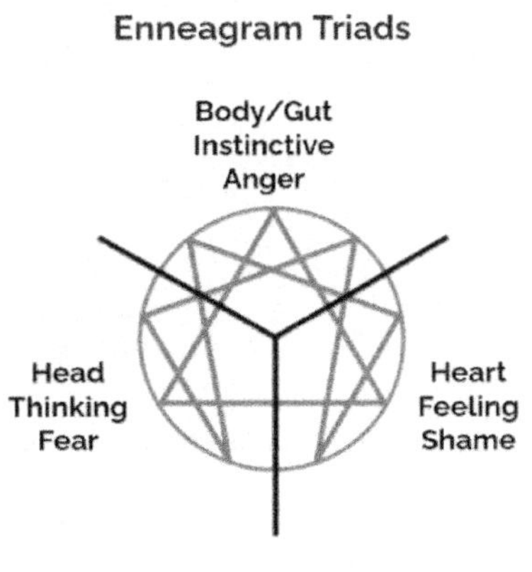

The Enneagram's personality Types are organized into three emotional triads, each representing a core emotional challenge: the Body triad (Types 8, 9, 1) processes the world through anger or repressed anger, the Heart/Feeling triad (Types 2, 3, 4) deals primarily with shame and image, and the Head/Thinking triad (Types 5, 6, 7) is driven by fear and anxiety. Each Type within these triads handles its core emotion differently—some express it openly, others repress it, and others move against it.

Type One: The Perfectionist Parent

- **Core Drive:** To be a good, correct, and exemplary parent
- **Basic Fear:** Being a flawed or inadequate parent
- **Basic Desire:** To be a righteous and improving influence
- **Key Parenting Characteristics:**
    - Strong sense of right and wrong in parenting choices
    - High internal standards for themselves as parents
    - Drive to improve family life and routines
    - Self-controlled and responsible approach
    - Attention to consistency and structure
    - Strong inner critic about parenting
    - Struggles with anger about imperfection
    - Natural ability to create order and routine
    - Values moral development highly
    - Difficulty with messy stages of childhood
    - May overly structure children's lives
    - Tends to correct and improve constantly
    - Challenged by children's natural chaos
- **Growth Path:**
    - Learning to allow natural development
    - Accepting imperfection in parenting
    - Softening critical tendencies
    - Making space for play and mess

Type Two: The Helping Parent

- **Core Drive:** To be needed and appreciated by their children
- **Basic Fear:** Being unwanted or unimportant to their children
- **Basic Desire:** To feel loved and valued as a parent
- **Key Parenting Characteristics:**
  - Highly attuned to children's needs and feelings
  - Warm and emotionally demonstrative parenting style
  - Strong desire to be important to their children
  - Difficulty setting boundaries with children
  - Pride in being an essential parent
  - Intuitive understanding of emotional needs
  - Tendency to over-help and enable
  - Natural ability to create emotional connection
  - May neglect own needs for children
  - Often over-involved in children's lives
  - Can become emotionally manipulative
  - Struggles with children's independence
  - Difficulty with healthy separation
- **Growth Path:**
  - Developing appropriate boundaries
  - Supporting healthy independence
  - Taking care of personal needs
  - Allowing natural consequences

Type Three: The Achievement-Oriented Parent

- **Core Drive:** To be successful and admired as a parent
- **Basic Fear:** Failing as a parent or having unsuccessful children
- **Basic Desire:** To feel valuable and worthwhile through parenting
- **Key Parenting Characteristics:**
  - Goal-oriented approach to child-rearing
  - Image-conscious about family appearances
  - Driven to help children succeed
  - Excellence expected in parenting role
  - Strong focus on children's achievements
  - Ability to motivate and encourage
  - Focus on external markers of success
  - Natural leadership in family activities
  - May over-schedule children's lives
  - Difficulty with children's failures
  - Tendency to push too hard
  - Struggles with just being present
  - Challenge accepting average performance
- **Growth Path:**
  - Valuing presence over performance
  - Accepting children's natural pace
  - Developing deeper emotional connection
  - Creating space for being versus doing

Type Four: The Individualist Parent

- **Core Drive:** To create unique, meaningful connections with children
- **Basic Fear:** Being an inadequate or inauthentic parent
- **Basic Desire:** To form deep, significant bonds with children
- **Key Parenting Characteristics:**
  - Emotionally deep and intuitive parenting style
  - Strong emphasis on authenticity
  - Highly creative approach to parenting
  - Attuned to children's emotional depth
  - Values unique expression in children
  - Rich emotional understanding
  - Appreciation for children's individuality
  - May dramatize parenting challenges
  - Tendency toward emotional intensity
  - Struggles with routine aspects
  - Can over-identify with children
  - Difficulty maintaining consistency
  - Challenged by ordinary moments
- **Growth Path:**
  - Finding meaning in everyday routines
  - Maintaining emotional balance
  - Creating stable structures
  - Embracing ordinary joys

Type Five: The Observant Parent

- **Core Drive:** To understand and be competent in parenting
- **Basic Fear:** Being overwhelmed by parenting demands
- **Basic Desire:** To feel capable and knowledgeable as a parent
- **Key Parenting Characteristics:**
    - Analytical approach to child-rearing
    - Strong need for personal space
    - Careful management of energy
    - Deep interest in child development
    - Values intellectual growth
    - Provides thoughtful insights
    - Preference for structured interaction
    - May maintain emotional distance
    - Struggles with emotional demands
    - Tendency to over-analyze
    - Difficulty with spontaneity
    - Challenged by constant needs
    - May withdraw when overwhelmed
- **Growth Path:**
    - Developing emotional presence
    - Balancing observation with engagement
    - Managing energy while staying connected
    - Creating comfortable intimacy

Type Six: The Security-Conscious Parent

- **Core Drive:** To ensure children's safety and security
- **Basic Fear:** Being unable to protect children from harm
- **Basic Desire:** To create a secure and stable family life
- **Key Parenting Characteristics:**
    - Loyal and committed to family
    - Strong focus on safety and preparation
    - Anticipates potential problems
    - Values reliability and consistency
    - Vigilant about children's wellbeing
    - Careful planning and organization
    - Strong sense of responsibility
    - May transmit anxiety to children
    - Tendency to overprotect
    - Struggles with uncertainty
    - Can be either fearful or rebellious
    - Difficulty trusting life's process
    - Challenged by letting go
- **Growth Path:**
    - Developing trust in life
    - Managing anxiety constructively
    - Finding balance in protection
    - Supporting healthy risk-taking

Type Seven: The Enthusiastic Parent

- **Core Drive:** To make parenting enjoyable and exciting
- **Basic Fear:** Being trapped in parenting difficulties
- **Basic Desire:** To maintain freedom while parenting
- **Key Parenting Characteristics:**
    - Optimistic and fun-loving approach
    - Creates adventure and excitement
    - Spontaneous and playful style
    - Focus on possibilities and options
    - Quick to find solutions
    - Ability to make things fun
    - Natural enthusiasm and energy
    - May avoid difficult aspects
    - Struggles with consistent discipline
    - Tendency to distract from problems
    - Difficulty with limitations
    - Challenged by routine
    - May miss emotional depth
- **Growth Path:**
    - Developing consistency
    - Staying present with difficulties
    - Creating healthy structures
    - Balancing fun with responsibility

Type Eight: The Protective Parent

- **Core Drive:** To be strong and protective of children
- **Basic Fear:** Being unable to protect or empower children
- **Basic Desire:** To ensure children's strength and independence
- **Key Parenting Characteristics:**
  - Strong and assertive parenting style
  - Protective of children's interests
  - Direct and clear communication
  - Strong sense of justice
  - Natural family leadership
  - High energy and engagement
  - Powerful advocacy for children
  - May be too forceful
  - Struggles with gentleness
  - Tendency to overwhelm
  - Difficulty with vulnerability
  - Challenged by subtle needs
  - May push too hard
- **Growth Path:**
  - Developing gentle strength
  - Balancing protection with tenderness
  - Allowing vulnerability
  - Creating emotional safety

Type Nine: The Peace-Making Parent

- **Core Drive:** To create harmony in family life
- **Basic Fear:** Creating conflict or disturbance
- **Basic Desire:** To maintain peace and connection
- **Key Parenting Characteristics:**
  - Peaceful and accepting approach
  - Strong desire for family harmony
  - Accommodating parenting style
  - Goes with the flow
  - Natural mediator in conflicts
  - Comfortable with routine
  - Patient and understanding
  - May avoid necessary conflict
  - Struggles with setting limits
  - Tendency to minimize problems
  - Difficulty being assertive
  - Challenged by decision-making
  - May merge with children's wants
- **Growth Path:**
  - Developing clear boundaries
  - Maintaining parental authority
  - Engaging constructively with conflict
  - Staying awake to family needs

Your Notes

About the Author

John Harper is a Diamond Approach teacher, a Certified Enneagram Teacher, and a spiritual traveler with over 56 years of experience. His journey began with a profound awakening in 1969, which led him to a lifelong exploration of truth, presence, and the unfolding mystery of existence.

For over twenty years, John has helped seekers explore the depths of their experience. Drawing on the wisdom of the Enneagram and the Diamond Approach, he helps individuals explore personality fixations and cultivate a deeper connection with their essence and true freedom.

His work is not about providing answers but opening the space for inquiry—for discovering what is real beyond conditioned patterns, beyond identity, beyond the known. Through presence, deep exploration, and engaged inquiry, he helps others navigate the inner terrain of truth, love, and self-understanding.

John is available for private spiritual inquiry sessions.

Contact: HarpGnosisBooks@gmail.com

Printed in Great Britain
by Amazon

62696608R00134